I was a victim of spring madness.

I hadn't realized how hideous I must have looked until one day a former boyfriend from a neighboring ranch came to call. He'd heard I was back and just "happened to be coming by." I was out in the brush hunting turkey eggs when he arrived. As I stepped out of a clump of chokecherry bushes at the side of the road, he slammed on his brakes and came to a grinding halt. I was dragging a kid by each hand.

   "Oh, John!" I cried in pure delight. He was the first person I'd seen in a week, and besides, he was a mighty nice guy. He stared at me, his face beginning to wilt like a bowl of last night's lettuce.

Can you die from pain? I clutched a bottle of ammonia that I'd been using for the youngsters' mosquito bites and took a quick sniff. Choking and gasping, I decided not to faint. Not yet, anyway.

The authors of the nursery tales, The Three Little Pigs and The Little Red Hen were completely ignorant of animal life in the raw. I could with great honesty rewrite the "Three Little Pigs" story and make the pigs the villains, hot on the trail of the poor terrified wolf. For pigs are like that, the ones I know, anyway. And I would enjoy doing over the "Little Red Hen" affair, when she was supposedly caught by a wolf and carried home to his wicked mother for dinner. The way I see it, the Little Red Hen was caught by a wicked little pig and eaten on the spot, without even the ceremony of sharing her with his mother.

If there's anything, to my way of thinking, more stupid and ornery than a pig, it's a bad-tempered turkey gobbler. And Brigham Young was certainly bad-tempered. I'd named him because of the number of wives, and not because of his disposition, however. Art once ventured to observe that anyone with that many wives was bound to be bad-tempered.

Other Books by Lucile Bogue

POETRY
Typhoon! Typhoon!
Eye of the Condor/Ojo Del Condor
Bloodstones:Lines from a Marriage
Windbells on the Bay
Smoke from Nine Lives

PROSE
Salt Lake
Dancers on Horseback
Miracle on a Mountain
I Dare You! How to Stay Young Forever

ONE WOMAN, ONE RANCH, ONE SUMMER

Lucile Bogue

Strawberry Hill Press

Strawberry Hill Press
3848 S.E. Division Street
Portland, Oregon 97202

Cover by Ku, Fu-sheng
Book edited by Kristi Burke
Typeset and design by Wordwrights, Portland, Oregon

Manufactured in the United States of America

Library of Congress Cataloging-in-Publication Data

Bogue, Lucile, 1911-
    One woman, one ranch, one summer / Lucile Bogue.
        p.   cm.
    ISBN 0-89407-121-1 (trade paper : alk. paper)
    1. Bogue, Lucile, 1911-   —Homes and haunts—Colorado.
2. Women authors, American—20th century—Biography.
3. Mountain life—Rocky Mountains. 4. Ranch life—Colorado.
I. Title.
PS3552.048Z468   1997
818'.5409—dc21
    [B]   97-18921
                                                              CIP

Acknowledgment

I acknowledge, with warm gratitude,
Lincoln-Herndon Press, Inc.,
for permission to include in this book the chapter
"Back to the Land," which originally
appeared in their book,
Treasury of Farm Women's Humor.

Dedicated to all those who
long to get back to the
simple life—
God help them!

TABLE OF CONTENTS

BACK TO THE LAND

April first was a warm and deceitfully beautiful day. Spring, real spring, does not come that early in the Colorado Rockies. But, of course, I couldn't be expected to know that. I had only spent all thirty-two years of my life living there. I was a victim of spring madness.

So, blithely and without mishap, the children and I covered the miles to our new life as country folks. I drove up the steep, winding red rock canyon with a joyous lilt of homecoming. The old ranch on which I had grown up was nearby, so every cedar tree and pine and clump of sage were familiar to me.

I noted with satisfaction as I drove up to the front gate that everything seemed to be under control. The log cabin had been stained a rich chocolate brown and the shutters and picket fence around the front yard sparkled clean and white. The lawn was showing spring green. My heart soared. It was beautiful!

The hens were cackling with spring-like activity in the hen house. The pigs were grunting with a sweet and gentle contentment in the pig pen. The two milk cows, who were soon to "come fresh," were grazing artistically in the greening hay field. A huge turkey gobbler, surrounded by an admiring flock of a dozen wives, preened and strutted about in front of the gate, his bronze feathers shining with the iridescence of a hundred precious jewels. Buff, a beautiful gold-and-white shepherd, bounded to meet us with joyful welcome.

Everything was perfect! Even down to a pair of bluebirds that fluttered and twittered about under the eaves of the cozy house. Harbingers of good luck. Yeah, the next time I listen to a pair of dumb bluebirds...!

"Ooooo...Mommie!" Sharon, 4, squealed in delight. "Look at the pretty doggie!"

"Ooooo...Mommie!" echoed Bonnie, 2. "Doggie!"

They were too intent upon the dog to observe the disaster that was overtaking them. I was just staggering out of the car, my arms loaded with a mountain of blankets and pillows, when I heard their terrified shrieks. I peered around the south end of a pillow just in time to see the attack. The gobbler leaped on them from behind, beating them to the ground with his heavy cruel wings.

I dropped the bedding and dashed to their rescue, yelling like a Comanche on the war path. But the dog was there ahead of me. The gobbler's blue mottled face turned fiery red as he felt Buff selecting a mouthful of his most choice tail feathers. The bird lifted himself a good six feet off the ground and soared across the barnyard with a thunder of wings and a flurry of disconnected feathers. Buff turned to me, grinning triumphantly, as he spat out a few surplus plumes.

I picked up the children from where they had been pounded into the earth, scraped the turkey manure from their knees and dresses, and examined the red welts on their arms and backs. With some difficulty I persuaded them that they would live and in time even recover completely.

Then we went to the house. I shall never forget the sight that met me as I opened the kitchen door. I have had some weird nightmares, but nothing that quite compared to that.

Eggs! Eggs! Eggs! In the middle of the kitchen table was a large zinc wash tub, filled to the brim with eggs. On the coal stove was a wash boiler, likewise heaped up. The work bench was laden with two large dishpans, fairly running over with eggs in varying shades of tan and pink. The floor was a maze of cardboard boxes of all shapes and sizes, filled with eggs.

It's incomprehensible what a couple of hundred hens can do in a few days if they really put their minds to it. I hadn't known there were that many eggs in the state of Colorado.

Sharon and Bonnie clung to my legs, their eyes widening in disbelief. Never, in all their lives, had they seen more than two dozen eggs at one time, and that was on Easter. Now their mouths were round O's of disbelief.

"Mommie," Sharon ventured in a very small voice, "God sure made a lot of eggs, didn't he?"

"He sure did, Pet!"

"You said we'd have tons of eggs. Is this tons?"

"Yes, I'm afraid it is. But I hadn't expected this many tons."

All my spare time for the next two weeks was spent with those blasted eggs. Those in the kitchen, to say nothing of the increasing horde that I kept carrying from the hen house to the basement.

The tragedy of natural egg production is that the darned hens are not at all fastidious. They don't produce eggs all ready to be dropped into the neat little cubicles of an egg crate. About half the eggs have to be cleaned first. Hens have utterly no regard for the poor fellow who has to clean and pack their output.

Of all the unpleasant tasks of farming, I soon decided, cleaning those damned eggs had to be the worst. I don't know how big-time poultry raisers do it, but I washed 'em. It was the only way I knew. I just dropped a batch of filthy eggs into a bucket of cold water and went to work with a rag, doing it by hand. Oh, God!

I once saw an ad in a farm magazine for a gadget that cleaned eggs automatically. It was an affair that sort of shimmied the egg around between two strips of rough cloth, guaranteed to de-dung an egg in nothing flat. But I was always a bit skeptical, and for the rest of my career as a farmer's wife, I continued to clean eggs in the primitive way.

But fortunately, ranch life was more than eggs.

I t all began normally enough. We were quite ordinary people, a young middle-class couple living in a small town in Colorado— one husband, Art, who was principal of the local elementary school; one wife, me, a former elementary teacher who was now a "mere housewife" busy raising two little girls, Sharon, 4, and Bonnie, 2.

The only thing that revealed a weakness in our apparent common sense was the fact that Art was consumed by a burning desire to become a "rancher." He hated his job in the classroom and dreamed of the heavenly freedom of nature in the raw. And my weakness lay in the fact that I had grown up on a ranch. I should have known better. I should have stopped him.

A faint sense of premonition kept kicking me in the ribs that day as I drove the two hundred miles to our new ranch, with Bonnie sleeping peacefully on the pile of bedding in the back seat, and Sharon chirping happily at my side.

My own memory of ranch life could not, by the wildest stretch of the imagination, be called a life of milk and honey (although we had a superabundance of both). Above and over everything always loomed the shadow of The Note At The Bank.

Dad wouldn't go to the big annual Strawberry Day Festival, because someone from The Bank might see him there, and think he was squandering his time and money, which all had to be applied on The Note At The Bank. I couldn't buy a perfectly ravishing blue glass necklace at the general store which cost twenty-five cents, because we had to save all our money to pay The Note At The Bank. Little sister Vernice debated long and bitterly over the choice between a ride on the ferris wheel and one on the merry-go-round because we couldn't afford to have both. Mom couldn't get a badly needed linoleum for the kitchen floor, because it would take all the available egg and cream money to finish out the next payment on The Note At The Bank.

And the gruesome thing about that danged Note was that it went on forever. Dad would march to the bank at regular intervals, with his head high and his face bearing the grim determination of an early Christian martyr walking into an arena of hungry lions. He would come out again, grinning in sick relief, his pocketbook empty down to the last penny. He'd made another Payment. Then he'd go back to the ranch to start slaving and scraping to do it all over again.

The Note At The Bank was a most unreluctant dragon. If you paid the required tribute, it wouldn't eat you. Not this time. It would back up a couple of inches and lick its fangs and snort fire at your heels, until the next Payment was due.

Art didn't know about this. There were also a few other little details he didn't know about ranch life. Such as the back-breaking labor of weeding the potato patch, or the way you feel when a bull gores to death the young work horse you just borrowed two hundred dollars to buy.

So even before Dad had called with "the opportunity of a lifetime," I had tried to deflect Art from his burning desire to become a farmer. One night, after filling him completely with meat loaf and mashed potatoes and apple pie, I took my teeth in my mouth and began.

"Honey," I inquired sweetly, "are you sure you'll like farming?"

"Of course I'm sure."

"Will you like pulling the weeds from a whole field of potatoes?"

He abhorred pulling weeds from even the tiny little garden behind our house. He had "a bad back" and wouldn't touch a weed with a ten-foot pole.

"I'll hire that sort of work done," he responded loftily. He settled back and away down deep in his easy chair and opened the evening paper, hoping to close the conversation.

"How will you like getting up at four in the morning to go out to irrigate?" I persisted. He was a natural-born late sleeper, "Or finish your milking chores at ten o'clock at night?"

For him, the period from supper on till bedtime was one of relaxation, pure and unvarnished. Nothing had ever jolted him out of it. It is a habit shared by a good many American males of the urban variety, but I think there are few who cherish it quite so passionately. I simply could not picture him kicking himself out into the cold cruel world for another three hours of milking, calf feeding, and various and sundry other chores, once he'd had supper.

"Hm?" he asked vaguely, from behind the paper.

I repeated.

"That's sheer stupidity, working all day and all night!" he responded in sudden anger. "I'll arrange my daily schedule so that sort of thing won't be necessary."

I was getting nowhere. Even I could see that. I took one last wild plunge.

"Darling, won't it worry you, being in debt and having the bank howling at your heels all the time? Not ever having a cent to spend?"

He lowered his paper and looked me straight in the eye.

"There's no need to go in debt." He sounded so darned sure of himself. It's hard to argue with someone like that.

"My folks were always fighting a mortgage," my persistence sounded weak. "All the farmers we knew were in the same boat."

"We're not going to be that kind of farmers." Period. That ended our discussion, as the newspaper went up again.

Well, every hog has to scald his own nose, Grandma used to say. Art was bound to become a Marlboro Man, and that was that.

And so we had gone on, planning to get a ranch some day. Art's and the children's enthusiasm had grown contagious. Even I began to bubble with exuberance when I talked about the baby chicks we could have, and the calves, and the oceans of milk and cream and butter and eggs.

And now I was actually on my way, alone with two babies, to run a ranch until Art could get away from school. Just two months during the spring rush! Nothing to it! Huh!

THE GOOD LIFE

It didn't take me long to settle down into the eventful routine of a rancher. "Settle down" might be too mild a term. Swallowed or inundated might be more accurate. I lost my own identity entirely. I became a slave to the whim of every whimsical animal on the place. And there were plenty.

I was unrecognizable, even to myself. After crawling through a few barbed wire fences, and dashing madly through the sage brush after a renegade cow, I learned that feminine attire just wasn't built for this sort of life. Sport shirts and gabardine slacks couldn't hold up under the strain. I solved the problem by donning a tattered pair of men's overalls I found in a closet, and a cast-off flannel shirt. After that the clothing problem was nil. So was my appearance.

I never was one to depend on a beauty parlor for my hairdo, but I had taken a kind of pride in keeping my hair gleaming clean and done becomingly. Now, some time between four a.m. and noon, I combed my hair. Some days. But often a crisis would arise that drove all thought of personal appearance out of my head. Combing...occasionally; shampoos and curlers were definitely out.

However, I was still the mother of two small children who had to be dressed, fed, napped, bathed, and put to bed at more or less regular intervals. I had previously considered that a full-time job. Running a ranch is another full-time job. Put the two of them together and you have a situation resembling Dante's summer vacation in Hell.

I hadn't realized how hideous I must have looked until one day a former boyfriend from a neighboring ranch came to call. He'd heard I was back and just "happened to be coming by." I was out in the brush hunting turkey eggs when he arrived.

As I stepped out of a clump of chokecherry bushes at the side of the road, he slammed on his brakes and came to a grinding halt. I was dragging a kid by each hand.

"Oh, John!" I cried in pure delight. He was the first person I'd seen in a week, and besides, he was a mighty nice guy.

He stared at me, his face beginning to wilt like a bowl of last night's lettuce. I must have looked ghastly. My face was red and sunburned and streaked with sweat. My stringy hair matted by the wind. In the ten years since John had courted me, I had grown considerably wider in the beam. And my ill-fitting male attire couldn't have helped much.

The children at the moment looked as bad as I. They were a couple of dirty little ragamuffins, tired and tear-drenched after a hectic trip through the brush. Nothing in our appearance suggested idyllic young motherhood.

"Hello," John finally managed a hollow greeting.

"Gee, it's good to see you again!" His coming was the first pleasant break I'd had, and I couldn't help sounding enthusiastic.

"Yeah." He looked like a trapped rabbit.

"How's everything going?" I primed him, trying to get him to talk. I didn't realize until that moment how lonely the past week had been.

"How's your mother, John? Is her rheumatism still bothering her?"

"Not much."

"Is Tony married yet?" Tony was his younger brother.

"No, he's in the Philippines in the Marines."

Our conversation faded for lack of support. Finally, after a crushing silence, he stepped on the starter.

"Well, I gotta get going. I'll be seeing you."

But he never did. That was the last time I ever saw him.

The major event of that first week was the birth of a bull calf. One morning I discovered that Mollie was missing from the hayfield. Old Blue was grazing, conspicuously alone.

"This is it," I thought, my heart sinking to the soles of my battered shoes. I'd known it was coming, for when a cow is expecting, nature is bound to take its course, sooner or later. But I'd been half hoping that if I ignored the situation, and pretended that it didn't exist, Mollie might forget about it and put it off indefinitely.

I hated milking. That is one of the things I was physically unequipped to handle efficiently. There are other jobs on a ranch which I am temperamentally unsuited to. But as for milking, I just wasn't born with what it takes. You need strong muscular hands, a substantial wrist, and plenty of oomph in the biceps. All of which I ain't got.

I used to try to milk occasionally when I was a girl, but sister Vernice could milk three or four "hard milkers" while I was trying painfully, by various and sundry contortions, to extract the lacteal fluid from the easiest milker in the herd. The last time I tried it, the long-suffering cow finally kicked me with such force, she sent me sailing halfway across the barn. After that, Dad didn't expect me to milk again.

Another angle worried me. Cows with newborn calves are often dangerous critters. They lose their gentle affability and become raging beasts. How I was going to go out into the woods with the youngsters, bring in the calf, and separate it from its unwilling mamma, I didn't quite know.

The children were terrified at being left alone while I went to another part of the ranch, so wherever I went, they went along. Sharon was a good little sport for her brief years and endured all manner of hardship for the privilege of going with me. But Bonnie had been walking only a few months, and her fat unwieldy little feet stumbled over every object she came to. I declare, she couldn't get her foot over her shadow without falling flat on her face. And each fall was accompanied by shrieks of wrath and despair. She didn't enjoy her hikes. Neither did I.

Despite difficulties, our calf hunt was successful. After three tortured hours, we came upon the polka-dot cow and her white-faced calf in the shade of a distant cedar. Hastily I shoved the girls under the low spreading branches of a pinon, much to Bonnie's vociferous disapproval. Pinon needles are stiff and very sharp. I left Sharon with strict instructions to stay under that tree, no matter what happened, and for the two of them to keep the trunk of the tree between them and the cow.

My knees were rattling a sixteen-measure break for castanets that would have done Xavier Cugat proud. I looked at Mollie. She looked at me. I took three uncertain steps in her direction. She took four steps in my direction, but there was nothing uncertain about them. We glared at each other with mutual distrust.

One of her horns was crumpled, and relatively useless as a weapon of destruction. The other was not. It had all the curve and point of a Russian saber. And about as much amiability. I moved stealthily from tree to tree, but I didn't fool Mollie a bit. She turned to follow my least movement with alert and angry eyes.

I stopped, in hopeless indecision. I was getting nowhere. I had to get that calf, come hell or high water. I simply had to! To leave the calf with the cow meant ruining the cow for milking, and I couldn't do that. That cow and her cream check were our bread and butter, literally.

On the other hand, I hesitated to make orphans of my children, especially while they were watching. If I were gored to death, they might huddle on that lonely hillside for a week, screaming, with no one to hear them. They would starve, perish in a storm, die of terror, or perhaps a combination of all three. The longer I contemplated that picture, the more undesirable it became.

I stood there, bathed in a lather of incertitude. To die, or not to die; that was what bugged me.

I was brought to my senses by a wail from Bonnie, down the hill under the pinon tree. She was tired and cold and hungry. I could hear Sharon trying to quiet her in her most efficient, four-year-old manner. But in another moment they were both crying.

That settled it. I had to finish this job and fast.

"Dear God," I murmured, "please make her horn soft."

I shut my eyes tight for a moment and then called to the children.

"Sharon, if anything happens to Mommie, take Bonnie home after it gets dark enough so that Mollie won't see you. Then call Aunt Vernie! Do you remember her number?"

"Yes...06J4."

I wanted to go kiss them farewell, but I hesitated to frighten them further. That would make it so final. Instead, I tucked my shirt tail down grimly into my pants and strode forth with long firm strides, straight at Mollie.

She stared at me in surprise. She tossed her head in my direction, with an angry slash of her horn. As I drew near, she began to fling the red sandy dirt up over her back with fierce hoofs.

"Hi, Mollie, old girl," I greeted her cheerfully but firmly. "I knew you had it in you!"

My teeth were chattering, but I wasn't going to let the old girl know it. I could have spent my entire life handling bovine maternity cases as far as Mollie would know. I'd like to think it was my confident demeanor that snowed her, but maybe she just sized up my petite five-foot frame and decided I wasn't much of a threat after all.

Thank God cows can't smell fear the way dogs are supposed to do.

I gave Mollie a sociable slap on the rump and bent to get the calf on his feet. He was a typical male, bullishly stubborn. He had no desire to stand, and no prodding on my part would budge him. Mollie watched me with some apprehension, but for the moment she kept her horn in abeyance.

I sweated and heaved. I put my arms around the calf's neck and tried to rise, his chin over my shoulder in an approved ballroom manner. No luck.

I crawled under his hind quarters and tried to raise him with my shoulder in his flank. He only relaxed contentedly and let me grunt and strain.

I resorted to words.

"Get up, you big buffalo!" I barked. "Shoo! Hoist! Scat!"

But he just lay there, a beautiful specimen of young bullhood, and looked at me with indifference.

I grabbed his tail and twisted it. I'd seen that done at a rodeo once, I remembered. I twisted until I heard the vertebrae crunching. He looked back at me in hurt surprise. That stopped me. After all, he was only a baby.

At last, in a fit of wild desperation, I did it. I'm ashamed to admit it now, but I did it. Yes, I bit his ear. I'd heard old timers say that's the surest way of handling an unmanageable horse. What works on a stubborn horse, ought to work on a stubborn calf, I said to myself. I tried it. The results were miraculous.

He leaped to his feet, and so suddenly that I had no time to dodge. My head was directly in his upward trajectory, but not for long. When a bull collides headlong with your face, something is bound to happen. I was sent spinning and found myself swimming lazily among the stars some distance down the hill.

Even my fingers could tell that my eye was rapidly turning black. By the time I could stagger to my feet, it was almost shut. That baby may have been young, but he sure had a head on him!

After that, it was easy. I shoved the mildly resisting calf half a mile to the corral, while Mollie breathed nervously down the back of my neck. I had an icy spot in the middle of my back where I expected the horn to pierce me at any moment. With a sigh of relief, I pushed little Ferdinand into his pen, and his mother into the barn. Then I ran back to the hillside to rescue my wildly sobbing babies. My first great victory!

SPRINGTIME
IN THE ROCKIES

In the old days, when you needed a hired man you went to town and entered Pinkie's Poolhall, the Pleasure Emporium. You'd walk up to one of the hungry-looking individuals lounging therein to ask if he was interested in a ranch job.

"Doin' what?" he'd inquire suspiciously.

"Oh, general ranch work. Driving a spud planter, drilling grain, and such like."

"No cows to milk?" Hired men always had a violent aversion to milking, a sentiment with which I was in deep agreement.

"No, I do the milking myself," you'd reassure him.

"O.K. What ya payin'?"

"Two dollars a day and board."

"O.K."

And he'd start out the door with you, his mouth beginning to water in anticipation of a good farm dinner. Then he'd stop suddenly in his tracks.

"Any ditch diggin'?"

"O.K. Four dollars, as long as ditch cleaning lasts."

But that was in the old days. When I began my personal career as a farmer, Pinkie's Emporium was as bare of prospective hired men as Mother Hubbard's proverbial cupboard. It no longer served as the local employment agency. No one, apparently, wanted to work, and especially work on a ranch. So farmers planted their own spuds and cleaned their own ditches and milked their own cows, as long as their strength held out. What they couldn't do alone was left undone.

The evening after I conquered the calf problem, the phone rang about eight o'clock. The girls and I were eating a meager supper of scrambled eggs and crackers. My back ached from carrying slop to the pigs, my legs ached from running up and down hillsides hunting turkey eggs, I was worried about the hens, whose egg production had fallen off fifty percent since my arrival, three of them had dropped dead besides, and I was hurrying to get the youngsters fed and in bed so I could get out to take care of Mollie and Ferdinand.

As I went to answer the phone, I felt more like beating it to bits with a hammer than talking into the blamed thing.

"Hello?" I managed a certain degree of frozen politeness.

"Say, the water's gonna be turned into the ditch on Friday. Reckoned ye'd want to know."

"Oh, thanks."

Water. Irrigating. More work. I'm afraid I didn't sound too enthusiastic.

"Got yer ditches cleaned yet?"

"Good grief, no!"

"Ditch cleanin's too heavy work fer a woman. Reckon ye'll jist hafta let it go fer this year."

I was too upset to summon a suitable reply, so the wire hung heavy with silence.

"Well," the neighbor signed off briskly, "gotta get to my chores. Remember, Friday the ditch'll start runnin'."

I don't know which is more diverting, ditch cleaning or a kicking cow with a caked bag. Both have plenty of bang when it comes to taking one's mind off one's inner self. However, I didn't have to make a choice. I had both.

Mollie's bag (udder, to you) became the size of a wash tub, a violent unhappy-looking pink, and as hard as a rock. Mollie was a most discontented cow. I'd heard "caked bag" being mentioned on the old ranch during my early years, and remembered that it eventually could become "milk fever," which is often fatal. But I couldn't recall any remedy.

I was scared stiff. I suffered with Mollie every inch of the way, for I'd had the same ailment in the maternity ward of a hospital. My treatment had been alternating ice packs and electric hot pad. But I could offer poor Mollie neither.

I tried milking her, but it did little good. It was like milking a turnip. I'd clutch a teat in both hands, and squeeze until everything went black before my eyes. Then I'd come up for air, and peer into the bottom of the bucket. There I'd find a few drops of the thick yellowish liquid, which after a few days would be followed by milk, if Mollie lived. This yellow stuff was needed by the calf, I remembered.

Mollie would endure my efforts for a time with patience. Then, when I was least expecting it, she would raise her foot with a quick little spang! and over would go the bucket, the milk stool, and me.

Then it was all to do over again. I knew that if I didn't keep at it, the cow would die and the calf would starve. By this time I would be quivering in every muscle from my toes to my ears, quivering with anxiety and physical strain. Poor Mollie! I'm sure I must have been a sore trial to her.

Each day the bag grew worse. The pink gave way to a feverish red. It continued to swell, although it had long since reached the stage where I expected it to pop wide open. It finally got so bad that Mollie couldn't walk. She could only waddle like an old goose, and not very far at that.

One morning at milking time I was going though the old routine before an expectant audience. The kiddies were standing against the wall of the barn, goggle-eyed with apprehension and delight. Around me sat a semicircle of hungry cats, patiently awaiting results. I was weeping silently into the milk pail, careful to keep my head buried in the cow's flank so the children wouldn't know.

In walked Joe. Dear old Joe. He was a neighbor I'd known when I was a little girl, a big, grey, shaggy mountain of a man, but oh, so gentle.

"Hello, girls," he addressed the three of us.

I gulped down my tears. I didn't want him to see what a fool I was.

"Oh, Joe! Am I glad to see you!"

"How's everything going?" I don't think I've ever heard a kinder voice. It had a way of making everything seem a lot better than it really was.

"Not very well, I'm afraid." I mopped the tears off the end of my nose with the back of my hand.

He came closer.

"Say, this cow's in bad shape, ain't she?"

"Yes. Do...do you think she'll die?"

He didn't answer. He ran firm gentle fingers over the feverish udder.

"What have you been doing for her?"

"Nothing...except trying to milk her. I didn't know there was anything else to do."

"Can you get me a little pail of warm water with some vinegar in it, and a soft rag?"

I flew to the house for what he asked, and in no time at all he was bathing the poor miserable bag. Mollie almost smiled, she seemed so pleased. Then, miraculously, he milked her. He got half a bucket full, where I'd been doing well to get a quart. He emptied it into the big pan in the corner of the barn where the cats ate.

"Oh!" I cried in consternation. "What's the calf going to drink?"

"We'll turn the calf loose with her for a while."

"Turn him with Mollie! I've nearly killed myself keeping them separated!"

"Oh, we won't leave them together. Just turn him in with her for a while night and morning, after she's milked. He'll have to work for anything to eat, and that'll work that bag down better than anything we can do."

What wisdom! Mollie kicked and flinched while Ferdinand butted that poor bag unmercifully. I'd never have dreamed of doing anything so cruel, but Joe knew best. He stroked her neck gently. When he finally put Ferdy back into his pen, Mollie's waddle was perceptibly improved. And at least a thousand pounds of anxiety had been lifted from my shoulders.

"I'll be back in the morning to see how she's doing," he said as he left.

Joe's visit left the day quite rosy. I found four more hens dead in the chicken house, and others were looking pale and listless, but even that didn't dent my cheerfulness. I would ask Joe about them in the morning.

I packed us a lunch, flung a ditch cleaning shovel over my shoulder, grabbed Bonnie by a fat little fist, and with Sharon trotting along beside, started up the mountainside behind the ranch. We even sang a little, before we ran out of breath.

I cleaned ditch. But I soon lost any enthusiasm, as day after day I whacked and cut and dug at great unwieldy lumps of sod that had grown in the ditch, stopping the flow of water. Straining with every muscle I had (which wasn't much, I'm afraid) I would try to pry them loose and lift them out. I gave up lifting them with the shovel, and finally got down on my knees in the ditch to start the clod moving, pushing with every available part of my anatomy, knees, thighs, hips, abdomen, chest. By the time I got it to my shoulder, the clod had reached the ditch bank. Over and out! And I was all in.

Then there was the little matter of brush roots which grew into the ditch. They would reach long hungry fingers into the water current, grabbing every bit of trash that sailed by, until they formed a sizable and disastrous dam. And if you think grubbing out iron-tough roots is a game for a lady, you have another think coming.

Aside from the above, there's nothing at all to ditch digging. Except rocks and wood ticks. Rocks are the odd-sized pieces of stony matter which livestock delight in kicking into the ditch as they graze nearby. I've never witnessed it, but I amused myself by imagination.

"Fore!" shouts an old plow horse, and raising a hind foot, lifts a rock off the hillside and neatly sinks it into the ditch with a plop. Some game!

As for wood ticks, they are the pernicious parasites which infest the countryside each spring, crawling onto their victims with no warning, scurrying to cover somewhere on your body before you can detect them. Then they begin their *banquet macabre*, which ends in death for the victim if you aren't lucky.

And so "ticking" became one of my daily chores. Every night before I put the children to bed, I would go over them thoroughly, inch by inch, hunting ticks. Have you seen a mother monkey in a zoo, de-lousing her offspring? That was me, overhauling each child from stem to stern. I would start by digging through their hair, strand by strand, and would end up searching between their toes.

Ah, springtime in the Rockies!

COME,
GENTLE SPRING

The days kept coming, one after another, balmy and beautiful, dawning a crisp blue, with scattered whipped-cream puffs of cloud, and ending at night with a riotous melody of rose and copper in the west. In spite of the many obstacles that farming puts in the way of a life of peace, there is nothing like a ranch on a hilltop for viewing sunsets. They were gorgeous.

But after the ditch cleaning started, my arthritis kept me in such misery that I couldn't have enjoyed a sunset if I'd taken a bath in it, or poured it over my potatoes for supper. Arthritis is just plain hell, and don't let any funny jokes about Grandpap's rheumatics make you laugh. T'ain't funny, McGee!

By the time the water was turned into the ditch, I was a wreck, much too old for my thirty-two years. But the ditches were cleared enough for the water to run. And the fun was only beginning.

Ditch cleaning is bad, but irrigating alfalfa is worse. This is due to two things, water and gophers. Water is the wonderful stuff. There's nothing like it for drinking, washing dishes, or bathing the baby. But when it comes to spreading it in an even flow across a very uneven field of alfalfa, it's not good. Definitely not good.

You can work for hours, digging and hacking to push the water along to those higher spots, only to find that the law of gravity has not yet been repealed. So you go at it again, searching for another route, working like a Marine digging a foxhole in a solid beachhead. And your joints cry aloud with arthritis.

Cold water doesn't do anything for arthritis, either. Anything good, that is. Honest-to-God farmers wear heavy rubber boots that reach to their knees. But I hadn't reached the honest-to-God stage yet, so I wore a little pair of woman's dress boots. When irrigating, the first thing I usually did was to go into the water over my boot tops, and for the rest of the day, I would slosh around merrily, carrying the cold water with me. Even my toes became rheumatic.

Gophers are the other factor that makes irrigating a most unpredictable game of chance. They are the diabolical little rodents which build a maze of tunnels under your hay field, taking a malicious delight in funneling off your water to the most unexpected and distant places. If you want a good stand of hay, it is vitally important to get that water to every part of the field. You work your fool head off, digging, cutting sod, building dams, only to find that your water has disappeared completely—as though by magic. If you listen carefully, you will hear a lively gurgling far down the field, where a healthy geyser is beginning to erupt.

G abriel Lifsky came over one morning to borrow some worm salts for his pigs. I didn't know worm salts from sweet essence of Come Hither perfume, but I didn't say so.

"I don't know as we have any," I told him doubtfully. "But if we have, you're sure welcome to it."

Gabriel was the Big Czech who lived just west of us. He must have been sixty years old, but he rode his black stallion with a dash that made him look thirty. Other nice things about him were a flowing mustache of the Gay Nineties era, a flashing white smile (too dazzling to be real, Art said), and a delightful command of broken English.

Gabriel had taken care of the ranch before I arrived, so he knew his way around.

"Ya, dere iss vorm salts, lots of him. I show you."

We followed along as he led us to the grain shed, Sharon, Bonnie, Buff, and I. He strode in among the sacks where I had been mixing chicken feed according to the formula tacked on the wall.

"You vill be having to go to town soon, sure. Your grain sacks, dey be almost empty, ya." And he began burrowing through a clutter of sacks, peering into each one as though he were expecting to find the worm salts. I didn't know what worm salts were, but I was sure they would not be found in a sack of oats or wheat.

"Ach! Here she iss!" he exclaimed, peering into a sack of meat scrap which I used in the laying formula for the hens.

"Oh, no. That's meat scrap."

"But Missus, she iss not! She is salts for de vorms in de hogs!"

He seemed to be very sure. That's the way with men, I thought angrily. It's hard to convince them of anything.

"I should know!" I argued. "Haven't I been feeding it to my laying hens, according to these directions, for two weeks now?"

"Feed dis stuff...to de hens?" His face seemed to turn slightly purple. "Mien Gott, voman...how much?"

"One of these small pails to a tub of grain, just like it says on the wall there." His superior attitude irritated me. I knew I was no farmer, but I could read, couldn't I? When it says one five-pound pail of meat scrap to a tub of grain, I guess I was smart enough to do that. Wasn't I?

"Your hens...how iss day doing?"

"Fine, thank you." I spoke with the icy hauteur of Mrs. Astorbilt's plush horse. He needn't be so high and mighty.

Realization suddenly struck me. Only that morning I had crawled under the chicken roosts to drag out two more dead hens, making a total of seventeen since I had arrived. The hens were not doing well at all!

"Oh..." I gasped. "Do you suppose that really isn't meat scrap?"

"Ya, sure!" He beamed with joy, now that he had convinced me. "Das vas vot I ban tellin' you! Dis is vorm salts for de pigs! Meat scrap, she ban gone t'ree, four veeks now."

"But...it did look like meat scrap." My rebuttal was weak but stubborn. "It's the same color."

The next morning I had to go to town. I was out of groceries. I was out of feed for the chickens, the turkeys, and the pigs. And I had come to the place where I had to sell some produce or move out. I had every egg case on the place full, all six twelve-dozen cases, besides two wash tubs and a boiler waiting for containers. I had to sell some eggs—or feed them to the pigs. And Mollie was really whooping it up in cream production. Both ten-gallon cream cans were full. A town trip was inevitable.

I awoke about 5 a.m. with a terrible premonition. I tried to turn over. An agonizing pain hit me in the neck and between the shoulders—one of my stiff necks. Someone must have hit me in the neck with an axe. I've had stiff necks before and since, but that took the prize. It's like having your head amputated without anesthesia.

I lay there, bathed in cold sweat. I had to get up. I had to dress the children and feed them. I had to milk Mollie and feed the calf and the turkeys and the chickens and the pigs.

With teeth clenched tight, I struggled out of bed. But as I started across the room, darkness started closing in on me and my feet and hands were a long way off. Can you die from pain? I clutched a bottle of ammonia that I'd been using for the youngsters' mosquito bites and took a quick sniff. Choking and gasping, I decided not to faint. Not yet, anyway.

The clouds that morning did not resemble puffs of whipped cream on a blue plate. They were wads of dirty sheeps' wool. A storm was brewing. Only damfools and tourists try to predict the weather, Dad used to say. But even a damfool could see what was about to happen.

By the time I had sweated my way through milking and stock feeding, a strong cold wind was whipping over the hills. And before I had finished loading the car with six immense egg crates and two cream cans, and had cleaned up the kids and myself sufficiently for urban viewing, rain was spattering down in half-dollar-size drops.

In town, the first thing I did was go to the drugstore, my head twisted over to my left shoulder.

"Give me the most potent pain killer you have," I croaked.

"What's the matter? Stiff neck?" the druggist grinned amiably.

"How can you tell?" I was not pleasant. "I've had eight aspirins. They didn't help. Hurry!"

He looked leisurely among the bile salts and hair tonic and finally handed me a bottle of liniment.

"Rub that on, ma'am. It'll fix you up. My wife swears by it."

"But I want something to take! Something that'll work fast!"

"Lady," he remonstrated, "if you've had eight aspirins, I'd advise against anything more taken internally."

I snatched the bottle from his hand, unscrewed the cap, and took a good swig. I remembered Old Bill, a hired man we'd had for years, who was always drinking "red liniment" to ease his miseries. After that one gulp, I knew why. His mind was so taken up by the molten fire within him, his other suffering seemed of no consequence. I think it was a mixture of rubbing alcohol and red pepper.

I walked out of the drugstore with the proprietor's eyes bulging.

The rain turned to sleet, and the children began to whimper with the cold. It was mid-afternoon before I had emptied the egg crates, sold my cream, bought the groceries, and loaded the car with four hundred pounds of grain. I was anxious to get home before the mud got too deep. I had childhood memories of mountain mud.

My memories were as nothing. The steep narrow canyon was no problem, for the road was red sandstone. But the last half mile was something else. If you've ever made a chocolate pudding and forgot to put in the second cup of milk, you know the sticky mess that results. Well...

Before we'd gone a yard in that yuck, I saw that chains were needed. So with stiff neck, rheumatism, my new sky-blue flannel coat, and a biting sleet storm, I lay down in the mud to attach chains to the rear wheels. I'd put chains on a VW once in a snow storm, but this was a different kettle of fish entirely. I wished fervently for the designer of that long sleek Chevy to drop by, so that I might shove his head in the muck.

With chains on, we slowly plowed ahead. The furrows grew deeper and richer, chocolate pudding rolling up on either side. Deeper and deeper...slower and slower.

The Chevy choked and died. Half a mile from home. Much, much later I staggered into the house, carrying Bonnie in my arms, all thirty pounds of her. And on my back clung Sharon, frozen almost stiff from the storm. I should have known that April would be like this.

This would be a good place to bring this episode to a close. But I must finish it.

After building a fire, peeling off our sopping garments, and getting into dry clothes, I tucked the children into bed with a hot iron at their feet and their tummies filled with coddled eggs and hot milk. Then I donned my farmer's garb, lighted the kerosene lantern, and started forth into the storm to do my chores. It was ten o'clock.

That was the night Mollie chose to be temperamental.

I couldn't blame her much. She was carrying around pretty

nigh a wash tub of milk which she was aching to get rid of. And she could hear her son bawling piteously. In addition, that storm was enough to make anyone nasty.

Instead of entering the barn door when I tried to drive her in, she zipped out of it like a bat out of a cave. The chase was on. She leaped the corral gate like the cow sailing over the moon.

I started after her at top speed, coattail flying and lantern swinging. Mollie took a gay turn out across the hayfield, bucking and kicking her heels, a la rodeo. I was sputtering worse than the lantern in the snow.

It was then that I hit the ditch. Down I went with an earth-shattering crash. Every joint in my body seemed torn asunder. I lay there for some time, groaning and trying to reassemble my scattered parts. The lantern had broken and in the pitch darkness the snow hissed against the hot glass.

When I finally staggered to my feet, the miracle had happened. The stiff neck was gone.

It was one o'clock that night before I finished the chores. The snow was three inches deep.

GOLDILOCKS

The telephone rang the next morning before I was awake. I groped my way over the icy floor. The world outside was buried under half a foot of snow. Winter had returned, despite the calendar.

"Hello." My tongue was still thick with sleep.

It was long distance. Fright jerked me awake.

"Say, where in the heck have you been? I tried all day yesterday, and until midnight last night to get you." It was Glenn, Vernice's husband. He went on, not waiting for an answer. "Dougie is in the hospital here in Denver, pretty bad. He was operated on for ruptured appendix yesterday morning. Vernice has to stay at the hospital with him and is leaving Glende with a neighbor. She's wondering if you could come down to get her for a couple of weeks until Dougie gets better. How about it?"

My breath floated across the kitchen in white clouds, while my heart sank.

Little Glende, Goldilocks, we called her, was a year-and-a-half old, just three months younger than Bonnie. And she'd never been away from her mother since the day she was born. I tried to imagine the complications. But I simply couldn't. I shut my eyes for a moment and took a big gulp of cold air before I could answer.

"Sure, I'll be down on that midnight train this evening. I can't make it any sooner, for I have a few little things to take care of first. But I'll be there. 'Bye."

I tried to sound very cheery and confident. Which I was definitely not. I thought of the car, buried in frozen mud and snow, half a mile from the house. I thought of the empty grain shed, and the hungry stock. And I thought of the children, whose entire wardrobe was in the laundry hamper, awaiting wash day.

The Denver and Rio Grande was just pulling out of the station as I scrambled aboard that night. My blood pressure must have topped 210, and my mud-splattered overshoes (the ones I used for irrigating) were flapping. But I was aboard.

I settled into a hard seat in the day coach with a sigh of relief. Everything was taken care of. I hoped. I had taken the children twenty-five miles up-country to the little town where Grandma Paddy-Cake lived. She was the postmistress and couldn't take care of them herself, but she'd find someone who could. And the livestock was under the firm supervision of my dear neighbor, gentle Joe.

There was just one thorn digging my conscience. I had ruined our big, beautiful, almost-new car. I'd driven the twenty miles to the train at feverish speed—with the brake on. The Chevy had no more brakes left than a plate of melted butter. The only way to stop was to run into a cement curb, I discovered.

After one jolting trial of my new method of stopping the car, I quickly realized it wouldn't be practicable for delivering eggs, or for driving down the steep narrow canyon from the ranch. I'd spent the last hectic moments before train time trying to rouse a mechanic of some sort.

The phone booth at the station acquired the temperature and humidity of a Swedish steam bath as I called number after number. It's astonishing how many reasons a mechanic can find for not being at home at midnight, or for not being able to work on a car the following day.

With my train tootling the signal to be off, I finally poured my message into a willing ear and dashed for the tracks. Just in time I leaped aboard, much to the impatience of the crotchety conductor.

Goldilocks was a darling. Golden curls, fat rosy cheeks, and chubby clinging arms, she was a perfect image of a cherub. And my adoration of her was returned full-fold. She accepted me without question, calling me "Mamma" along with my own.

But therein lay the rub. A feud soon developed between Glende and Bonnie over my affections. Twins are a fine institution when they are raised from birth as such. But I soon realized that it didn't work out so well if they've lived for their first eighteen months as The Baby.

Sharon and Bonnie had never been rocked to sleep. It was a lovely custom if you have time for it. But it seemed I never had. On the other hand, Goldilocks had never gone to sleep without the lulling influence of a rocking chair.

"O.K.," says I to myself with resignation. "If she has to be rocked, I'll rock her, by golly!"

So I sat myself in the rocking chair with Glende on my lap and rocked, and rocked, and rocked, fuming inwardly at the thought of the hours of work still waiting for me by lantern light outdoors. Sometimes she was easy. Fifteen minutes would do the trick. Other times it was an hour, or an hour and a half. If I tried laying her down before she slept, she developed a case of screaming hysteria.

So while I rocked, I listened to the hogs howling ravenously in their pen, and Mollie and Ferdinand bawling an unhappy duet over the corral fence. I have always regretted that I am not a calm, easy-going person. When I die, it will be from a stroke brought on by high blood pressure, I'm sure. And the events of that summer didn't prolong my life.

All went as well as could be expected, until Bonnie discovered Glende's technique for going to sleep. Then the war was on. She was her Mommie's baby, poor little dumpling, and she wasn't about to have some Johnny-come-lately muscling in on her territory. Bonnie's howls won out. I was forced to rock them both simultaneously.

I came to two conclusions. First, that a woman can handle three small children successfully alone. Secondly, that a woman can operate a small farm successfully alone. But a third conclusion forced itself upon me. A woman cannot do both at the same time. I did both, but the success rate was sub-zero.

After Goldilocks came to live with us, wash day became imperative. I had managed to forestall it for a month now by rinsing out a few articles in the wash basin. But with two babies to wash for, rinsing was definitely out.

Wash day dawned bright, and as clear as a baby's eyes. I got up at four-thirty in order to get an early start, and had the chores and breakfast finished by nine o'clock. Four hens had hatched their turkey eggs that morning, and so it was half past ten before I got the new arrivals transferred to coops in the turkey pasture. But even that was reasonably early. I felt pretty good about it.

I hauled bucket after bucket of water out of the cistern (the pump being out of order) and filled a wash boiler on the stove to heat. The clothes were sorted, mountains of them, and piled about the kitchen floor. I filled the fuel tank of the gasoline washer, filled the tub with hot water, soap, and clothes, and stepped on the starter.

I stepped on the starter. I stepped on the starter. I had been assured that the machine was in perfect running order, yet nothing happened. I stamped violently on the starter. It required a queer combination of muscles that began to ache with my exertions. It's a killer of a setting-up exercise.

You raise your foot knee high and push the starter to the floor with all you've got. I tried it, again and again. My water was getting cold and my temper hot. Yet still nothing happened.

I choked it. I was so angry that I could have choked it with my bare hands, but I did use the little lever clearly marked "Choke." To no avail. The thing wouldn't even cough.

I called the Ford mechanic in town and asked him for advice. My dander was up. I'd started the washing, and by thunder, I was going to finish it! He told me what to do about the feed line. I did it. Nothing happened.

I called a hardware store that sold washing machines. They told me how to test the spark. I had only the vaguest idea of how to follow the man's technical-sounding instructions, but I did it. It sparked beautifully. So that wasn't it.

I called a neighbor who had a gas washer, and asked her for advice. She told me to call her son who lived forty miles away. He always fixed hers when it wouldn't work. I called him, but he was out in the field. His wife would have him call when he came in.

I waited impatiently. Time passed. I fixed lunch for the children. Still no phone call.

The suds in the washer had long since grown cold. And I, with idiotic determination, had gotten to the state where nothing could stop me. Nothing. I was going to make that blankety-blank-blank washer run.

I had set it up on the open-roofed back porch in order to avoid more crowding in the kitchen. Now I stood, alternately glaring down at the diabolical *bête noire*, and up at the rapidly gathering storm clouds. My legs were quivering from the repeated pumping of the starter, and I noticed with some regret that I had broken through the floor boards with the violent kick of the starter pedal.

But events never came singly or serenely at Park Hill Ranch. They came in bunches, and with distressing effect. I chanced to glance out across the field.

There, in front of God and everybody, stood old Bluey with a newborn calf. Another calf! It would have to be brought in and separated from its mother. (And this time I would have three children along.) Another tub of milk to extract from a fresh cow. Another caked bag, probably. It was too much.

I took the wrench I had been working with and flung it at the machine with shameful violence. I wish that I could say that thereupon it started off as though by magic. Or, to make it even more dramatic, that the entire thing fell apart before my eyes, repaying me for my fit of temper. Nothing at all happened. There was just one small dent in the washer.

Sometime, about midafternoon, the lad from up country returned my call.

"Do you know anything about machinery?" he asked.

"No," I admitted, "not a blamed thing. This is the first time I was ever closer than the steering wheel to a motor of any kind. But I'm going to make the blasted thing run. Just tell me what to do."

"O.K.," he laughed. "You asked for it. But I'm telling you, it's no job for a lady. Now here's what you do." And he was off in a wild jargon of armatures, lock washers, timer screws, spark plugs, etc.

Under normal conditions, I would have fallen apart in utter confusion. I don't understand machinery. I detest machinery. And what's more, I don't want to have anything to do with it. But these weren't normal circumstances. So I listened attentively, memorizing every word he said.

Within half an hour I had the entire motor apart and spread

out neatly, piece by piece, on the porch. My knuckles were bleeding and my hair down in my eyes, but I knew what I was doing. The children were sadly disappointed that I gave stern warning that they were not to play with any of these exciting toys. I had to keep an eye of constant vigilance on them.

I reassembled the whole thing, with nary a spare part left over. Still it wouldn't run.

I called Aunt Judith. She had been a fixer from everything from earaches to broken sleds ever since I could remember. She could make a darling doll from an old sock, or could make paint from alkali mud and skim milk. She was wonderful. Maybe she could help me. She listened to my account patiently.

"It sounds like fuel trouble," she said with a calmness I'd always admired. She made things sound so pleasant and easy. "Are you sure it's gasoline you're using?"

"Why...I guess so. It's in a big red five-gallon can with the word 'gasoline' across the front. It smells like gas."

"Pour a little on the ground and light a match to it. You can tell that way."

I tried it. It was about as combustible as pea soup. I smelled it. It still smelled like gasoline. Then, for the first time, I noticed two words scrawled faintly across the can with pencil. It said "Cleaning Fluid."

The rains came. I was on down on my knees trying to drain the fuel tank. The only hose I could find was too old and collapsible to work as a siphon. So I was doing it the hard way, sucking and spitting.

At that moment a powerful gust of wind blew the screen door open with a bang, hitting me in the head with a blow that would have cold-konked a horse.

That was the last straw. I sat down flat on the porch, with the rain running down my neck, and sobbed. It was the first time in their lives that the girls had seen me cry.

"Poor Mommie," whispered Sharon, creeping into my arms.

"Poor Mommie," repeated Bonnie, creeping in, too.

"Poor Mommie," echoed Goldilocks, her arms around my neck.

After that, life didn't seem quite so revolting.

PIGS IS...!

As a child, I remember hearing of a book called *Pigs Is Pigs*. I never read it. I wish I had. Perhaps it would have given me a deeper perception of pig psychology. As it was, I can think of a dozen different words I could apply to a pig, and not a one of them is "pig."

"Wolf" might be the most genteel of them. The authors of the nursery tales, "The Three Little Pigs" and "The Little Red Hen," were completely ignorant of animal life in the raw. I could with great honesty rewrite the "Three Little Pigs" story and make the pigs the villains, hot on the trail of the poor terrified wolf. For pigs are like that, the ones I know, anyway. And I would enjoy doing over the "Little Red Hen" affair, when she was supposedly caught by a wolf and carried home to his wicked mother for dinner. The way I see it, the Little Red Hen was caught by a wicked little pig and eaten on the spot, without even the ceremony of sharing her with his mother.

Pigs will eat everything and anything, in absolutely limitless quantity. Here's a true story Uncle Jess used to tell. One morning he filled the hog trough with milk fresh from the cream separator, with several inches of thick, air-whipped foam on top. The pigs waded in as usual, each trying to outdo the others in gulping it down with frantic speed. He hadn't got far from the pen then he heard a loud report, something like the blow-out of a tire. Dumbfounded, he returned to investigate. There, stretched out beside the trough, lay one of the gluttons, his side of bacon blown wide open by the pressure of milk and foam.

Hattie and Sal never filled themselves to quite that degree, but I think it was only because they were older pigs, and their hides were tough enough to withstand the pressure. They roared morning and night for their victuals, and when I was a little late, they almost tore the log pen down trying to get at me.

I spent half my waking hours feeding them, or listening to

them bellow for food. Twice a day I carried slop to them, a five-gallon pail apiece, filled with soaked grain, milk, and vegetable peelings. As these buckets were too heavy for me to carry, I hauled them to the pen in the kiddies' wagon. Traversing the rocky terrain with the contents of the buckets intact was a trick I never quite achieved.

Then would come the excitement. Hattie and Sal lunged wildly at the top log of the pen, their foaming snouts just over the edge. I was terrified that they would break out at any moment. They outroared any lion in the zoo at feeding time while the three children watched from the safety of a nearby hay rack, their little faces white and tense.

Here is the procedure for feeding the beasts: With a heavy club, you bang the critters across the schnozzle. This is a necessary safety measure, designed to insure your own life, and to distract them for a few seconds. While they back off to nurse a pained snout, you clamber up the side of the pen with a small bucket and begin ladling slop into the trough with frantic speed, for those devils will be back at you again. And with your toes poking through the logs, you have plenty to lose. Pigs love raw meat.

You must keep the club handy and keep battering in order to get the slop into the trough. If you don't, the damned fools will knock the bucket out of your hands, or stand in the trough and let you pour their repast over their backs. Haven't I read somewhere that a hog has the smallest brain per pound of body weight of any living animal? I believe it.

In addition to the slop, I had to cut a bushel basket of fresh weeds, hay, or grass each morning for them, using a mean little tool known as a grass hook, which resembles the sickle displayed on the Russian flag. If it's not razor-sharp, it won't cut anything, and if it is, it will cut through anything, from a pinon tree to your own thumb.

That's what happened one morning, almost severing my left thumb. And did they appreciate my sacrifice? Not a bit of it, except that I think they did enjoy the taste of the fresh flowing blood before I could stanch the wound.

Perhaps I should have been more sympathetic with their "delicate condition," as I had been told that they were expecting, and would produce a new crop of piglets any day from May first on.

"You have to eat for two now," Grandma used to admonish ladies who were "that way." If Grandma was right, Hattie and Sal were expecting litters of twenty each.

May wore on, and still no piglets. But I was so busy I didn't worry much. The thing that did worry me was their chicken dinners. I thought there seemed to be an awful lot of feathers in the pig pen, but then, there were chicken feathers everywhere in the barnyard. It was to be expected, with so many hens running about.

One day, as I was shoveling and mixing a tub of food in the grain shed, I heard wild childish screams from the direction of the pig pen, and the frenzied barking of faithful Buff. Terror struck at my vitals. I plunged for the scene of horror, still grasping my shovel.

I found all three children on the hay rack, hysterical with shock. And in the pen was Sal, calmly chewing the leg of one of my best laying hens, who was trying desperately to escape. I leaped into the pen and started banging Sal across the back with my shovel. But not for long. She whirled on me, her mouth wide, blood and froth dripping from her great tusks. She charged, with the snarling roar of a killer.

I have never been noted for agility, but the way I cleared that fence must have been beautiful to see. It was over and out—with Sal gnashing slivers from the log at my heels. My knees were as weak as branch water, but I still had both legs.

Sal turned grimly to her chicken, who was trying to drag herself to safety. Hattie was nosing in close, hoping to share in the chicken dinner. But one swing of Sal's wicked tusks changed her mind. I stood helpless, frozen at the ghastly event, as Sal began at the tail and crunched her way through the hen's innards. The poor creature continued to squawk in agony until she disappeared down Sal's throat.

Now, do you see why I could rewrite the story of The Three Little Pigs?

Old Sal had her pigs the day poor little Bon-Bon took down with the measles. Bonnie woke up that morning, "being sick" all over the place. And from the way Sal acted, she would have "been sick" too if she'd been able. For once she was not interested in food. But with Bonnie's temperature soaring to 103.5, I didn't care much about Sal's confinement.

Poor Goldilocks didn't appreciate the extra attention I was giving Bonnie. Glende had been getting the big edge of my spare time and love, because she was the baby of the trio, and a long way from her mother. But now that Bon was so ill and needed all the time I could give her, Goldilocks' baby soul burned with righteous indignation. She'd show that bad old Bonnie! And she did, every time I left the house.

I left Sharon in charge of things while I did the chores, but efficient as she was for her four years, she was not enough to cope with the two little feudists. So on my next trip out, I took an unwilling Goldilocks with me. The two couldn't be together, but they couldn't bear to be separated, either.

The next day, with Bonnie half-delirious with fever, old Sal half-dead but still no piglets in sight, and Goldilocks shrieking her disapproval at my failure to rock her to sleep, I was forced to admit defeat. I just couldn't hack it any longer.

I phoned Glende's paternal grandmother and asked them to come get her for a few days until things thinned out a little. And I called the veterinarian out from town to see what he could do for Sal. There had been time then I wished I'd never have to look down the snout of that ugly beast again, but now that I saw the imminent possibility, I was frightened. We couldn't afford to lose that sow and a litter of pigs.

"Too bad, too bad," the vet shook his head solemnly, weighing each word he uttered. "A fine brood sow. But you should have called me sooner. After two day's labor, she doesn't have a chance." Then he turned brisk with authority. "You'll have to get that other sow out of there right away, you know."

I thanked him for his kindness and asked the fee.

"Only fifteen dollars," he said, as though he were offering me a bargain.

Fifteen seemed a pretty steep price for looking at a dead pig, but I worked off my ire by building a partition in the calf pen and transferring a rebellious Hattie to new quarters. This project, interrupted by frequent trips to the house to sponge Bon's feverish little body and build up the morale of her loyal nurse took the rest of the day.

That night before I went to bed, I took one last look at old Sal. She had ceased groaning. I wondered how I was going to dispose of the corpse in the morning.

But the vet didn't know Sal. She was too stubborn to die. The next morning there she lay, grunting gently, with twelve little pink-and-black piglets rooting at their self-help breakfast.

Pigs is...well...pigs.

BRIGHAM
YOUNG

W hen we arrived at Park Hill Ranch, the first animal to greet us, you will remember, was a ferocious turkey gobbler. If there's anything, to my way of thinking, more stupid and ornery than a pig, it's a bad-tempered turkey gobbler. And Brigham Young was certainly bad-tempered.

I'd named him because of the number of wives, and not because of his disposition, however. Art once ventured to observe that anyone with that many wives was bound to be bad-tempered.

Brigham lost no time in teaching us all a lesson in caution. That initial attack on the youngsters was just the beginning. Every time they ventured out of the front yard, he flew at them, battering them to the ground with his powerful wings. If Buff was near enough to hear their cries of distress, their rescue was assured. There was nothing which pleased him more than to be allowed the privilege of selecting a mouthful of Brigham's tail feathers. And Brigham didn't stay around to argue. He was as stubborn as he was mean, and he would fight a human to the last ditch. But let Buff grab a mouthful of the old boy's winter underwear, and he would rise in the air like a balloon full of hot helium and fly halfway across the ranch.

Sharon, from the depths of her four-year-old wisdom, soon learned not to leave the yard without her body guard.

"Here Buffy! Here Buffy!" I'd hear her calling, and I knew she was about to go out.

Brigham had no more respect for adults than he had for children, I discovered. His battle procedure was invariably the same, a surprise attack from the rear.

One day I was engrossed in the act of stirring a bucket of grain and slop for the hogs, forming a nice target as I stooped. Without warning, I was suddenly knocked flat by someone with a club. My first thought, as I went sprawling over the slop bucket, was that I was being murdered by one of the neighbors who had gone berserk. Then, with his feet raking me and the thunder of his wings beating me over the head, I recognized my assailant.

I managed to get back to my feet, dripping with slop and boiling with anger. Before he knew what I was doing, I jumped straddle of his back. With one arm around his neck to keep him from getting away, I slapped his face until he was dizzy. He was as strong as a young ox, and the ride he gave me was a wild one. But for once I was able to show him what I thought of turkeys.

That incident should have "larned him his lesson" but it didn't. It merely served to throw oil on the roaring flame of his hatred of humans. He would hover around the back gate, waiting for a victim. Then he would follow along behind with a waltzing, sidling movement, waiting to catch us unprepared. Someone must have told him about the *pièce de résistance* of Thanksgiving dinner.

One afternoon I discovered a big nest of chicken eggs in the doghouse. I tried to rake them to me with a stick, which didn't work. The only way to get them was to crawl in after them. I was halfway in when the attack came.

No air raid siren, no bells ringing, no warning of any kind. Just the bombing, sudden and obliterating. Brigham beat me, and raked me, and lashed me and clawed me—the part protruding from the doghouse. I tried to crawl in, but I could only get so far. Too much hip and not enough door.

I bellowed for Buff, but apparently he was out in the field, hunting gophers. Even though I howled at the top of my lungs, I couldn't be heard outside the doghouse. It was like yelling down a rain barrel. The effect is terrific for the one doing the yelling, but it doesn't go very far.

And all the time Brigham was beating me and raking me with his cruel spurs. I was afraid to crawl out, for fear he would beat my head to a pulp. I kept yelling for Buff. The air in the doghouse grew stifling, the temperature of a good hot oven. My bellowing had used up all the available oxygen. Conditions at both ends of my anatomy grew steadily worse.

About the time I was sure I couldn't survive another minute, there was a great swoosh behind me, and Brigham was gone with the wind. Buff had come to my rescue, and not a moment too soon.

The dog's aversion to turkeys was almost as violent as the turkey's was to humans. Buff had finally gotten to the place where he didn't wait to perform a rescue. He tore into Brigham any time it occurred to him, always emerging from the attack with a grin and a mouthful of turkey feathers. The only thing he liked about gobblers was the swoosh they made as they left the earth.

I tried to curb Buff's activities. After all, Brigham had a necessary biological function to perform and he needed a little peace and quiet in which to do it. But it is hard to explain to a dog when he should bite a turkey and when he should not, so I was kept busy either calling him off, or sicking him on.

He finally became so confused that he began chasing the turkey hens as well as Brigham. Anything dressed in turkey feathers was on his list. One day I glanced out the window just in time to see a hen sailing down over the hill with Buff close behind. By the time I reached them in the gulch a quarter of a mile away, he had her down. Feathers were flying everywhere. He was having a grand time plucking her.

It was then that I decided Brigham must go.

The egg laying season was about over, for it was now nearing the end of May. Brigham's tribe had increased by about sixty poults, although for the time and effort he put into the undertaking, there should have been ten times that many.

I had reaped a harvest of about two hundred fifty eggs, representing about that many hours of egg hunting out of the best years of my life. Raising turkeys is the hardest way to make a living of any I know. They are absolutely uncooperative, from the egg on through adult stage. In fact, they prefer to die in infancy than to grow into a Thanksgiving dinner.

The trouble starts just gathering the eggs. A turkey hen is an artist at deception. To make a nest, she picks out the most unlikely spot she can find, high on a hill along a ditch bank, down in a gulch under a mass of tumble weeds, or along the road in the exact center of an impenetrable mass of oak bushes. After laying her egg each day, she covers it with grass and leaves so that one wouldn't see it if he walked over the top of it.

Your only hope is to let the hen lead you to it, and that is the last thing in the world she intends to do. If she sees you watching her, she will go in any direction except to her nest. It takes a lot of subterfuge on your part to keep her in sight without looking at her. About the time you think you're getting pretty sneaky, you steal a quick glance in her direction. She has disappeared entirely.

It becomes quite a game of skill and can go on for hours, usually ending by your getting tired and quitting, for once she gets out of sight, you may as well throw in the towel. But if you are persistent, and very, very clever, you may eventually track her to the nest. The only thing in your favor is the fact that when a turkey has an egg to lay, it simply must be laid. She can't hold on to it forever.

I kept up this daily game of hide-and-seek for two solid months. About the time I would locate a nest and hope to collect an egg from it each day, the old bird would get wise and move to a new location. Any time you try to pit your wits against those of a turkey hen, you'll come out the little end of the horn. Multiply that hen by twelve, and you can see the problem I was up against. But I didn't have sense enough to give up. We needed every nickel we could earn if we were to survive as ranchers. Whenever I saw a turkey heading for the hills in a businesslike manner, my nose began to twitch like that of a bloodhound on a hot trail, and I was off again.

Out of the two hundred fifty eggs I gathered, I managed to hatch a bare one hundred, setting them under chicken hens. The neighbors tried to comfort me.

"Turkey eggs jest ain't hatchin' good this year. Bill says it's because there's spots on the sun."

"You ain't the only one. Ever'body is havin' trouble with poor hatches."

"This jest ain't the year fer raisin' turkeys, I reckon. Some years is good. Some years ain't."

"It could be because you put 'em to set the wrong time of the moon."

I didn't know where the fault lay. Brigham had done his duty, the hens had done theirs, and I did mine the way I saw it. Despite all that, the turkey crop was poor.

But finding the eggs and hatching the turks was only the beginning. A baby turkey can find more reasons for giving up the ghost than a dog has hair. You feed him a little too much, and he dies. You feed him not quite enough, and he dies. He walks in wet grass, and he dies. He gets chilled in a cold snap, and he dies. During hot weather the old mother hen's lice get bad, and he dies. He wanders too far from the coop, gets friendly with a hungry coyote, and he dies. He gets curious about the bullsnake that loves young turks, or he gets his foot hooked up in the wire netting of the fence, and he dies. Didn't I tell you?

When I finally decided that Brigham was no longer indispensable, I called a restaurant in town and made arrangements to have his remains delivered at thirty cents a pound. I planned the execution for a day when Vernice could be visiting me. She had the strength of an Amazon, and a Yankee ingenuity that could solve anything. I had no idea how I could kill and dress the critter alone, but with her assistance, anything was possible.

First we put Buff into the yard and locked the gate. Then I walked boldly into the barnyard and stooped over (having made sure that Vernice was near at hand). Just as Brigham flew at me, I whirled and made a wild lunge for him. Slippery feathers skidded through my hands, but somehow I got hold of a huge horny leg. I held on.

The effect couldn't have been worse if I'd grabbed the hind leg of a bucking Missouri mule. My arms were jerked from their sockets. I hit the ground like a ton of brick, but I hung on with everything I had.

He spread his great wings and set sail, with me as anchor. He couldn't attain quite his usual elevation nor speed, but he was doing all right, considering the interference. I was not doing so well, skating around the ranch in a prone position, peeling off vast areas of skin on every available rock.

Then Vernice overtook us. She jumped astride Brigham, pinning down his wings. We shouted for her son, Dougie, age 5, to bring on the ropes. We tied one around Brigham's neck, hangman fashion, another around his feet.

Once we had him tied up, we argued long and heatedly over which of us should swing the axe that would behead him. Finally Vernice was convinced that she must do it. I had tried chopping the heads off chickens, but my aim was invariably off center. I either chopped off its beak, or struck it about halfway down its back. Either way was not good. And this would be bad enough at best.

We got the end of the rope around his feet thrown up over the cross arm of the hay stacker and hoisted him into the air, feet first, his wings beating like flails. While I held him suspended, she pulled the other rope and stretched his neck across a horizontal log which we were going to use as a chopping block.

She told Dougie to pull the neck rope tight until she could swing the axe. He held it a moment, his eyes wide in terror. Then, just as she swung, he dropped it and ran sobbing to hide behind the haystack. It was all more than he could bear, poor child.

Brigham swung free, battering me with his mighty wings, unscathed but indignant. We tried again. This time we got Sharon to hold the rope. She was so tiny, we were afraid she didn't have the strength. But she said she could, if she could shut her eyes and turn her back on the proceedings.

Vernice swung the axe and the deed was done. Brigham had joined the immortals.

Sharon turned to look at us and began screaming. Bonnie looked at us and began screaming. Glende looked at us and began screaming. Dougie came out from behind the haystack and began screaming, too.

We looked at each other and almost joined the chorus. A gorier spectacle we'd never seen. Streaming blood from head to foot, we looked as though we were the victims of the execution. But it was turkey blood.

When we got him dressed, Brigham weighed just thirty-nine pounds. Try that one in your electric broiler.

Brigham is gone now. One mustn't speak ill of the dead. But there is one thing I feel compelled to add. I don't like turkeys. Except on a platter.

A KINGDOM
FOR A HORSE

The one form of animal that was lacking on Park Hill Ranch was horses. As a rule, plowing and such like was hired done by someone with a tractor. When horses were really needed, such as at potato planting time and haying, they were borrowed from a neighbor in return for a few days' work. Our predecessor had told us that the farm was too small to warrant the year-round upkeep on a team, as they were used only a few days. This way was much better...the man said.

There was a small hand tractor to use in cultivating the garden and berry patches. It was marvelous—if you had the strength of a Belgian mare and a thorough knowledge of gasoline motors. I had neither. I never was able to get the blamed thing started by myself. And after it was started, I hadn't the size nor the physical oomph to direct it where I wanted it to go.

The tractor would start putt-putting out across the landscape, cutting a wide furrow through the middle of the strawberry patch, raspberry patch, corn patch, and cucumber vines, with me clinging desperately to the handle bars. It could go through a chicken wire fence as though it weren't there. The only means I found of stopping the blasted thing, unless I could remember in the press of the moment which gadgets to push and pull at the right times and in the right order, was a deep-set boulder directly in its path, or some similar object, such as a chicken house. A horse will stop when you shout "Whoa!" This tractor wouldn't.

Art's school was out the last week of May. He arrived at the ranch, all glowing and shiny-eyed, just in time for potato planting. I had already arranged the spring plowing with Joe, and so the field lay waiting, with the warm earth moist and mellow in the sun. Art was like a young colt turned out to pasture, fresh and unbroken. His enthusiasm was contagious. With him taking the burdens of irrigating, milking, calf feeding, and hog feeding off my shoulders, I felt as though I were on a vacation at full pay. I even had time to take a bath and put my hair up. It was wonderful.

We celebrated his arrival by the ceremony of cutting potatoes for planting. He dragged sacks of potatoes out of the cellar so we could sit in the balmy sun as we worked. He arranged a couple of old car cushions for us to sit on, and then, with paring knives and potato baskets, we went at it.

"Man! This is the life!" he gloated, stretching his feet out comfortably. "This beats the school-teaching racket a thousand ways! Sitting out here in the fresh air...the sun warm on your back...the bees buzzing around...bluebirds twittering in the eaves...the kids making mud pies...and our own bit of good earth under our feet!"

I had a cynical remark to make about each of his romantic observations, but sensibly I kept them to myself.

"Mm-hm," I assented tactfully. With things as they were at this moment, life did seem beatific. I could almost forget the ditch digging, and the sick pig, and the rheumatism, the gophers, Mollie's caked bag, and impassable mud. It's marvelous what having a man around the place will do for you.

We cut potatoes and we cut potatoes. We had no idea how many potatoes it would take to plant the field Joe had plowed for us, so we asked him. We very nearly passed out on the spot when he told us, but we were not about to let a few hundred pounds of cut potatoes stop us on the threshold of the Great Adventure. It was fun...at first.

Later in the day, the sun got hot and Art dragged the potatoes back into the dark cellar where it was cool. We chatted gaily about our plans for the future. As the afternoon wore on, our chatter ceased. Our fingers became blistered and raw, with mud and potato juice running into fresh cuts. Our knuckles became so stiff we could scarcely wield our knives.

Now I know what a service man means when he groans about K.P. duty, with spuds to peel by the hundredweight. The only difference between our job and a marine's was that he removed the skin from the tuber, while we counted the "eyes" and then carefully divided the potato into four to eight pieces, depending upon its size and the number of its eyes. I don't know which is more stimulating, our job or the G.I.'s, but after the ten millionth potato, it didn't make much difference.

I t was the horse problem that really stymied us. There wasn't an available team of horses within a radius of fifty miles. We asked Gabriel. He was using all his horses and didn't think he could let them go until some time next November. We couldn't hold off on potato planting that long. We asked Joe. He didn't have any horses. He had only a tractor, cows, and a Ford pick-up. We asked Chuck Harris, who didn't have any horses either, and he was booked up weeks ahead with his tractor. We asked a neighbor named Tilley, but he'd just lost one of his work horses with colic. He was in as bad a spot as we were. Said he guessed he'd have to harness his wife along with his other horse to get his spuds planted.

"Oh, give me a horse, a great big horse..." Art begged piteously in his sleep.

The cut potatoes began to rot. We started feeding them to the hogs...our precious potatoes upon which we had expended so much blood, sweat and suffering.

Then Tom Haskell's boy was taken suddenly sick and had to be rushed to the hospital for hernia surgery. That left Tom in a fix, with no one to ride the back end of his spud planter and only half his potatoes in the ground. So he and Art made a deal: He would lend us his team and planter if Art would lend him a few days' work.

First we planted Tom's crop. Everything worked fine. The fourth night Art came driving up the canyon on an Iron Age spud planter behind a gorgeous matched work team. He was as pleased as Punch, you could tell by the way he sat up tall and slapped the lines across the horses' backs. Our farming had really begun.

I believe, looking back on it, that everything would have been all right if that had been a one-man planter. But it wasn't. An Iron Age is as satanic a piece of farm machinery as man ever invented. One fellow sits in front, driving the horses. His partner sits on the seat behind the hopper, with a sort of revolving pie pan in front of him. This pan has a ring of two-inch holes in the bottom.

The idea of the contraption is this: As the potatoes come tumbling out of the hopper into the revolving pan, they are supposed to drop through a hole, one at a time, and down the tube that eventually buries them in the furrow. The catch lies in the potatoes tumbling down in overwhelming batches, while the back-end man works like crazy trying to shove a potato into each hole as it comes around.

And God help the man who has his finger in a hole as the plate revolves! The slickest way in the world to lose a digit. That wheel keeps turning relentlessly, no matter how many fingers you sacrifice to the God of Spuds.

Next morning as we started, Art drove the horses, powerful, spirited young brutes they were, while I was the "end-man" on the back seat. Either job was bad for an amateur, especially one whose eyes kept wandering out to the edge of the field to check up on the children. But I was grateful that Art would rather drive that team than eat fried chicken on Sunday. He loved those huge, high-lifed horses.

At first I found it rather fun. I've always been a "patternist," with an aptitude for fitting things into their proper niches. It was a fascinating game, sorting those spuds at top speed, getting one into each hole. Zest was added by that ever-present element of danger. You grab for a spud that is out of place, only to have it drop into the wrong hole. It takes a pretty quick trigger finger to keep from getting "bit."

I soon learned, however, that this was no job for a gal with hay fever. The field had lain plowed too long in the sun, and the soil was powdery dry and heavily dusted with dandelion pollen. The horses' hoofs and the planter stirred up a dense cloud that engulfed me.

I sneezed. I wheezed. I choked. I gasped. I wept copiously, utterly out of control. With emotional tears, one eventually runs dry. With allergy tears, there is no end in sight as long as there is anything to weep about. Blinded, I continued to sneeze and sniffle.

By noon my vision had become so liquidated that I could scarcely see a horse in front of my face. I could have been twenty thousand leagues under the sea for all the potatoes I could see in that pan.

After dinner we decided to change places. Art hated to relinquish his beloved horses, but he agreed that the dust was not so bad up front. I was scared to death of those great, prancing horses, but I wasn't going to let him know it. As I took the driver's seat, I felt as helpless as if I had been put in control of the Queen Mary and told to take her from New York to Liverpool. I knew that with my ignorance and lack of brawn, there was little I could do about controlling the behavior of my steeds. I could only hope that their desires would coincide with mine in all matters of importance.

The first day ended triumphantly. With the sun pouring red-gold fire over the fields and cedar hills, I drove back to the barn. Art followed along behind with Sharon, Bonnie, and Buff. As I turned the team over to Art at the barn door, my fear left me, and in its place was a feeling of expansive well-being. Almost half our potatoes were in the ground. My heart slid back down my throat where it had been all afternoon and settled into its usual position with a gentle thug, thug.

The next day followed the same routine. My heart jumped back into my throat the minute I took the lines, but I assumed a look of bright self-assurance which I hoped would conceal my desperate helplessness from Art. Steadily, the planting progressed. It was with satisfaction that we noted, as we turned at the end of each row, the lengthening patch of potato furrows, and the dwindling patch of open ground. When we stopped for noon, we estimated that we could finish that night if we worked until dark.

That afternoon was the longest one in my life. An iron seat on a piece of farm machinery is absolutely the hardest object in the world. I mentioned this fact to Art as we paused at the end of a row to fill up the hopper with more spuds.

"Truer words were never said," he groaned, stroking the seat of his farm overalls tenderly. Poor boy. Just a week out of the schoolroom. He eyes were red and almost blind from the dust, and I was sure that a certain part of his anatomy was as blistered as mine from the continual beating administered by those iron seats.

"Maybe we'd better stop now," I ventured. "It must be nearly six o'clock. See where the sun is. We could finish in an hour in the morning."

"I can stay with it if you can. I'd like to get it finished, wouldn't you?"

"O.K. Dump your spuds in the hopper and let's be on our way. I'm sure the kids have finished the graham crackers and are starved."

"I intend to lie on the front lawn tomorrow and sleep all day," he announced as he dumped the potatoes.

"Wouldn't it be great to heat a wash boiler of water and have a good bath?" I mused longingly.

I could hear shrieks of discord from the youngsters at the edge of the field, where I'd planted them and a few toys on a blanket with the suggestion that this was their playhouse for the day. Bonnie, dirty and tired and dissatisfied with the setup, was toddling out across the rough plowed ground, falling at every step. Sharon was conscientiously staying within the confines of the "house," screaming and pleading with Bonnie to return. It was no life for two babies.

Another hour and we'd be done! My eyes turned longingly to the finish line, the end of the field. I was tired, Art was tired, and the children were sunburned and irritable and worn to a frazzle. We should stop. But we were so near the end.

"All set?" I called over my shoulder.

"All set."

"Giddap!" The horses jumped against their collars and surged ahead. The dust rolled up from their feet and from the wheels of the planter in a heavy rust-colored cloud. We were on the home stretch.

A few moments later a terrible cry erupted from the back of the planter. I jerked the horses up short and turned to find Art twisted over the machine in agony. When I ran back to him, he was just yanking what was left of his finger out of the revolving iron plate. The flesh was torn from the bone from one end of his finger to the other, leaving the bone bare and white. It was a moment before the blood began to flow.

I don't know what we said or did, but we started out for the house, walking mechanically. We were halfway across the field when we heard it. At first it didn't penetrate the stupor we were in. And then, with the thunder of their hoofs almost upon us, we turned and saw them.

It was a runaway. The horses, with the planter careening wildly behind them, were lunging ahead across the field with mad blindness, shooting past us in a cloud of dust.

The children! Where was Bonnie? My heart stopped completely. For a time my entire body ceased to exist. The dust cleared enough for me to see Sharon, still on the blanket, unharmed. But Bonnie was not to be seen. My baby. My precious baby.

For a moment I even forgot Art and the mangled finger. I raced across the field, frozen in terror, to where I could see a bit of pink lying between the furrows. Bonnie had been wearing pink.

There she lay on her face. As I approached, she sat up, sobbing, rubbing the tears on her dirty little cheeks.

"Mommie, I'm hungry!" she wailed as I snatched her up and kissed her in relief.

She was unhurt, a few feet from the deep path cut by the plunging hoofs. Weak with relief, I called to Sharon to follow and ran for the house. Somehow I got the kids into the back seat of the car and Art and his bleeding hand into the front.

The trip to town broke all previous speed records. I saw assorted wheels from the Iron Age planter scattered across the country, a quarter of a mile of barbed wire fence torn loose and stretched across the road, and several pickets from the front yard fence lying up on the hillside among the pinon trees. But I didn't stop to investigate the outcome of the runaway. That could wait.

We left the kids in the car and staggered into the waiting room of the community hospital. A nurse appeared when I rang a bell and inquired what we wanted. Blood was flowing from Art's hand and down over his clothes.

"A doctor, please" I asked, "before he bleeds to death."

She nodded politely and left us. A few minutes later she returned with a mop and sopped up the widening pool of blood.

"Isn't there a doctor we can reach somewhere?"

"Yes, ma'am. He'll be here before long. Just have a seat."

She left. Art was looking whiter by the minute. It seemed that the least she could do would be to let him lie down somewhere. After a while she came back with the mop and mopped up the puddle of blood again.

"Won't the doctor be here soon? We ought to get this bleeding stopped."

"It won't be long now. He's eating his dinner. He'll be here as soon as he's through." She left us a basin to catch the blood.

She left again, to wring out the mop, I suppose. If Florence Nightingale could have seen that gal that night, she would have thrown in the sponge.

Half an hour later, the doctor appeared, jovial and well-fed.

"Hi, fella!" He slapped Art cheerfully on the back. "What were you trying to do? Use your finger as a meat substitute?"

He led him into the operating room, gave him a shot of something or other in the arm, and proceeded to sew the finger back together again, what was left of it. It took eleven stitches. I watched the operation, holding Art's tossing head and stroking the hair back from his cold wet forehead.

A strange far-away feeling began to envelop me. The doctor had finished dressing the wound and was beginning to swathe the hand with bandages, when my field of vision decreased to the point that I could see only through a tiny peephole in a gray curtain.

With high drunken steps I headed for the door. I didn't make it. The next thing I knew, I woke up on the operating room floor with a cold wet towel around my neck, wondering where in the hell I was.

Did I say "A kingdom for a horse"? I should have said, "The whole darned potato crop for a horse." When we harvested the spuds that fall, we sold them for almost half enough to pay Tom for a new potato planter and a set of harness.

THERE'S BOUND
TO BE KITTENS

I don't know what they called him before we came to the ranch, but we named him Butch. He was a huge square-built cat with a big head, big feet, big jaws. Everything about him was built for wear and tear. If he had been a human, and you had met him on the street, you would have taken him for a prize fighter.

There were a dozen other cats gathered in the barn at milking time, but they faded into wan insignificance when Butch appeared on the scene. It was easy to see that he was cock of the roost. When he sauntered in the door, the others eyed him warily. Silently, the group parted to allow him to take his accustomed place at the cow's heels. And when the warm milk was poured into the big flat pan, the others gave him plenty of elbow room. They had learned the hard way. He had a temper like a bear with a sore tail.

His was a case of schizophrenia. With others of his species, he was as sociable as an African lion on half rations. But with humans, he was a pussy cat. He would rub vigorously against your legs with his motor purring full speed. He would bound along the path ahead of you like an exuberant puppy. He loved the youngsters. At first I warned them to leave him strictly alone. He was so big. And I had seen him lash out with a wicked claw at the other cats.

The first thing I knew, Bonnie was dragging him around in her arms in a state of limp contentment. And Sharon found him infinitely more satisfactory than a doll. She spent a good part of her time dressing him in her doll's coat and bonnet and wheeling him around the place in her doll buggy.

That was Butch during daylight hours. Ah, but the nights! If you think that city-dwellers have a corner on alley amours and midnight yowling, think again. In a city, cats are usually distributed at the rate of one cat to about twelve dwelling units. At Park Hill Ranch, the ratio was reversed, twelve cats to one unit. This translates to plenty of sleepless, screech-riddled nights. And to think that we were here for the peace and quiet of country living.

"Lovers' lane" was the space under the front porch, which, incidentally, was under our bedroom window. Those cats could have courted and mated, undisturbed, in any of a hundred other places on the ranch. But night after night we would be aroused from deep slumber by a din of yee-owling and thumping and fftting. And night after night, armed with righteous anger and a broom, Art and I would dash out in our pajamas to break up the noisy party. You'd have thought they would learn. But there were so many of them.

As we would swing the broom around under the porch in an effort to hit one of the howling lovers, various and sundry cats would shoot out through the holes in the lattice. And often, if we would swing long enough, Butch would eventually come bounding out, his eyes blazing in the darkness. He resented this invasion of his privacy and every erect hair, from his neck down to the end of his bristling tail, was an exclamation point to that effect. His long fur made him appear twice as big and twice as fierce when it stood on end. At these moments I was half afraid of him myself. He was ready to scratch out the eyes of anyone or anything within reach.

Art finally rebelled at this nightly partying. He was never one to be aroused from sleep cheerfully.

"It's either Butch or me," he growled one morning when the five o'clock alarm called him up from a too brief sleep. "One of us must go."

"Oh, it's just the mating phase," I hastened to placate him. "It will pass. They'll forget about it after awhile."

"Maybe they will, but a few more nights like last night and I won't be here to see it."

I knew it was useless to argue. When he was in a bitter mood, there was not much to be done about it. Besides, I felt almost the same way myself. Those midnight serenades were beginning to frazzle my nerves, too.

"What's more," he groaned, down on his knees to retrieve his shoes from under the bed where he'd kicked them off at three a.m., "if they keep this up, we'll have a hundred and forty-four kittens around here to feed before long."

Our future, with one hundred forty-four kittens, didn't look too bright. Here was a problem worth worrying about.

"We've got to get rid of Butch," he growled as he turned and stamped irritably down the stairs.

But it wasn't the caterwauling nor the prospective kitten crop that finally did Butch in. It was his growing fondness for baby chickens and turkeys in his diet.

At first I wasn't sure. More than once when I went down to the chicken pasture to look after the baby chicks, I found him slinking away through the weeds with none of the proverbial bravado of the cat who ate the canary. I wasn't positive what he was up to, but it was obvious that he didn't want to be caught in the act. He must have had an unpleasant experience along that line in the past.

And then, looking out the kitchen window, I began to find him in the turkey pasture, sitting in front of a coop and watching the little turks, fascinated. I would rush out, yelling, to send him kiting in a cloud of dust. I wasn't about to wait to see if his intentions were truly honorable.

Then one day, I heard a baby turkey squealing. I dashed out to find Butch crawling through the fence with a young turk in his jaws. I flew at him, bellowing like a mad woman. He looked at me in hurt surprise, dropped the turkey and fled into the weeds as though the devil were after him.

That did it. I agreed with Art. Butch must go. But of course we couldn't let the children know. We decided that the execution would take place early in the morning, before they woke up.

Next morning we got up, depressed by the thought of what lay ahead of us. When I got down to the kitchen, I found Art with his .22 in his hands, a picture of utter dejection.

"Are you ready?" he asked in funereal tones.

"Do I have to come?" I argued. "Can't you do it alone?" I couldn't go out there with him to witness Butch's murder.

"Come on." I knew by his tone that he wouldn't budge until I went with him. I went.

We found Butch curled in his favorite morning spot, a sunny place in the path to the johnny-house. His white paws were folded neatly under his chest, his eyes closed, and he was wrapped in a smile of beatific contentment as he lay basking in the early sun. He was a picture of elegant innocence.

Art sighted down the barrel of the gun. Butch was a perfect

target, motionless, squarely facing us, and too close to possibly miss. Slowly Art let the gun sink to his side.

"Gee, I hate to wound the poor old guy," his voice was hoarse. "I'm afraid I'll botch the job."

"Go ahead!" I was anxious to get it over with. I was beginning to feel a little sick. "Go ahead. You can't miss."

Again he raised his gun and sighted. I froze, waiting for the shot. Again he let the gun sag at his side.

"What will the kids say when they find out?"

"They won't find out. You can take him off and bury him on a hill somewhere before they ever wake up," I told him impatiently.

"Here," he brightened with sudden inspiration, shoving the gun into my hands, "you do it. You're a better shot than I am, anyway."

I recognized the subtle flattery and the touch of the cold steel made me shiver. I drew back in panic.

"No...no! I couldn't in a million years!"

"Aw, come on. Yes you can. Remember how you used to pick those .22 shells off the bushes?" he wheedled.

"Oh, but I couldn't shoot Butch! It would be like shooting one of the kids!" I cried in horror.

"But that's what you're expecting me to do!"

"You're different. You've killed lots of things with the gun... deer and rabbits and things. You're used to it."

"Scared, huh?" His voice was contemptuous. "I thought you were the gal who wasn't afraid of anything!"

"I'm not scared. I just can't do it, that's all."

He thrust the gun into my hands and patted me encouragingly on the back.

"Come on," he coaxed. "Show your old pappy what you're made of. Now, that's it. Draw a close bead. Remember it's a pretty short distance."

I looked at Butch's serene face over the bead of the gun. He opened his eyes and looked at me, a wide questioning look like the ones the children gave me at times. My heart gave a cold flip-flop. I pushed the gun back at Art with frantic haste.

"I can't." I shuddered at the thought of what I had almost done.

Then we heard the voices of the youngsters inside the house, laughing and chirping like awakening sparrows.

"Hurry, before they get out here!" I urged.

Speedily he drew bead and fired. Butch uttered a muffled cry, jumped high into the air, and fell back to earth, kicking spasmodically. I grabbed a cardboard box and Art thrust the *corpus delicti* inside.

"Here, hide it in the coal house until this afternoon," I whispered. "You can bury him while the kids are taking their naps."

That evening at milking time, a figure paused a moment in the barn door, then sauntered in. The cats broke ranks respectfully to allow Butch to take up his usual place at the cow's heels.

Art stared, his eyes bulging in disbelief.

"Butch! Good God....!"

The only mark that Butch had to show for his recent execution was a small neat crease extending from a spot between his eyes back to the top of his head.

We didn't try it again. Butch had earned his reprieve.

Several weeks later, I was called from the garden by the excited screams of the children. Their little faces were wild with rapture.

"Mommie! Mommie!" They were standing at the barn door, jumping up and down in a state of joyous hysteria. "Come and see what we found!"

When I arrived at the scene, there was Butch curled in a nest in the manger hay, nursing a family of kittens.

Poor Butch! She had been a lady right from the start!

LET THERE BE LIGHT

One of the most enlightening things about our return to the good simple life was the lack of light. We found that we could fight mud and snow and turkey gobblers and gophers and drought and runaway horses. But in the long run, the things that really got us down were the little things, like finding the water bucket dry when we were thirsty, or hunting for a light switch when we entered a dark room and then remembering that there was no electricity.

For me, it was the light mostly. When I first came to Park Hill, I wore the pattern off the wallpaper beside each door, hunting for the light switch. It took me a long while to learn. It seemed I was always in a hurry, and when you're in a hurry, it's much worse. You can't imagine how wonderful civilization is until you leave it behind and move to a ranch without electricity or running water.

I'm not talking about all the nice farms and ranches equipped with running water, boiling and iced, electric conveyors to carry slop to the hogs, and reading lamps for the hens. I'm speaking about the rural places where the magic of electricity and running water have not yet reached, where everything is done the hard way, by the sweat of your brow and the crick in your back, as it was done by Great-Grandpap and Abe Lincoln.

One of my most vivid childhood memories was the advent of gasoline lights in the ranching community where I grew up.

Mrs. Martin brought a gasoline lamp to furnish light at the Christmas program at the little one-room school, the first of these new-fangled inventions any of us had ever seen. The two kerosene wall lamps which had heretofore lighted such proceedings suddenly faded into the shadows. Up until that moment we had considered their fluted tin reflectors and brass brackets quite the classiest thing in lighting equipment. I can remember gazing at them dreamily during arithmetic class, and wishing with all my heart that we could have a lamp like that at home.

But when Mrs. Martin came marching into the school room that night with the gasoline light hissing and fuming in all its pristine glory, kerosene lamps became instantly passé. We blinked in its sudden brilliance, and our mothers warned us in excited whispers not to look at it directly or we would go blind. But we noticed that the mammas and the pappas stared at it, fascinated.

A delightful thrill of tenseness was added to the occasion by the fact that a few days before, little Glenn Martin had come to school looking like a singed chicken, with nary a sign of an eyebrow or eyelash left, and his tow head burned almost bald.

"I wath watchin' our new gath light," Glenn lisped his explanation. "We wath all thittin' around the table after thupper and I wath real clothe watchin' the light, and all of a thudden it went whoof! And the fire began thootin' up to the theiling and the firtht thing I knowed I didn't have any hair left."

The story had spread through the community like wild fire, and so everyone sat on the edge of his seat, ready to make a mad dash for the door at the first warning of a "whoof." The children's songs and recitations received only divided attention that night, for it was the lamp that stole the show.

It behaved beautifully until the last scene of the Christmas pageant. The chubby primary youngsters, draped in sheets, were lined up on a bench in the background to represent angels. Myrtle Blue, likewise swathed in sheets, enacted the part of Mary, looking quite beautiful, a far cry from the clumsy twelve-year-old who usually went about stumbling over her own feet. The big boys, garbed in their daddies' bathrobes, were Joseph and the shepherds.

I was reading the Biblical script as my part of the performance, when I was stopped short by a sudden change in lighting. I froze stiff. Then it came, the "whoof" everyone had been expecting. Yellow flames burst out of the lamp and climbed in a steady stream toward the ceiling.

Some of the folks began squawking like a coop of scared chickens. Others, like myself, were so scared they couldn't have opened their mouths if they'd tried.

Most of those who could yell could also run, and there was a mad scramble for the door. The door wasn't nearly wide enough. The Virgin Mary jumped headlong from her chair and landed flat on her face, with a herd of terrified little angels on top of her. Joseph and the shepherds made for the exit like frightened jackrabbits, despite the bathrobes. They would have made it, too, if they hadn't run afoul of Uncle Jess. It just happened that he was carrying the flaming torch out the door and they couldn't get past.

After the excitement had subsided and the lamp resumed its customary sizzling, everyone trooped back into the schoolhouse, stamping the snow from their feet and crowding around the stove. The consensus seemed to be that the lamp wasn't such a bad gadget after all, in spite of its temperamental ways. Folks began to ask how much the blamed thing cost, and where you could get one like it.

It wasn't long before the entire community became gasoline lighted. When at last we bought a lamp of our own, it was with a delightful sense of opulence that we sat down at the supper table with the thing hissing brightly. We had stepped into the New Era.

But that had been years before. After living for years with lights at the flick of a switch, it's hangman's fun to go back to the old ways.

I would come staggering into a dark house at night with two buckets of warm milk, trying desperately to remember where I had left the lamp the night before. With a handful of matches I would start in search. By the time my supply of flickering lights was almost gone, I'd find the lamp upstairs in the bedroom.

I couldn't light the blasted thing where I was, because I had to go back down to the kitchen in the dark to get the pump. I would feel my way down the stairs in Stygian blackness, falling over the piano stool, and kicking over a bucket of turkey eggs I'd intended to set under a hen that night.

At last I'd reach the kitchen cupboard and the pump. With a simple twist of the wrist, I'd try to open the valve to pump the air pressure in. I'd try. I'd try again. Then I'd give up and begin hunting for a pair of pliers or a wrench, with the aid of more matches. Accompanied by a steady flow of muttered vituperation, I'd finally unearth a wrench and open the valve.

Then I'd begin pumping. I'd pump and pump and pump. I'd count...twenty-one, twenty-two, twenty-three. It said, with the directions that came with the lamp, that twenty-five strokes was sufficient. I tried that once, producing a light of approximately one-fourth candle power. I'd go on pumping...fifty-six, fifty-seven, fifty-eight...

About the time I'd feel sure that I would never be able to draw another normal breath, and that my arm would wither away because of a ruptured tendon or something, I'd stop pumping, hoping that this would be enough air to last part of the evening, at least.

Then came the lighting. I'd hold two lighted matches against the generator to get it warmed up, breathing a prayer meanwhile that the matches would hold out long enough to do the job. They seldom did. Ah! This time they did, by a split second. I'd hear the fizzle... that meant that the gas was cooking. The matches were getting shorter and shorter, but by sheer will power I'd determine that I'd hold them until the thing lighted. But will power had little to do with it. The matches would curl, burn to the end and break off.

With my fingers scorched to a crisp, I'd start all over again with a fresh pair of matches, and at last get the infernal thing to blazing properly.

Now I'd be ready to take the milk to the basement to the milk separator. But I could carry only one bucket at a time, because I'd have to have the other hand free to carry the lamp. As I'd make my second trip downstairs, the lamp would fade and go out.

The gas tank must be empty, although I couldn't see how in the world it could be. It was filled last night...wasn't it?...and it "shook" as though it had plenty of fuel in it. It was always tough to decide whether to venture the rest of the way to the basement in the dark with the milk and an empty lamp, or go back and start all over again. I'd decide the latter.

Much later I'd wend my way down the basement stairs, this time with a full lamp blazing beautifully, and with a bucket of cold milk upon which the cream had already set. The process had occupied the space of half an hour. See what I mean by the advantages of electricity?

Running up and down stairs to look after the youngsters at night could be eventful, too. Those were war years and flashlight batteries couldn't be had for love nor money. We slept "up" and the girls slept "down," so I usually kept a kerosene lamp burning all night in order to be ready for any rush call from below stairs. These cries of urgency averaged two or three a night.

One night, blind with sleep, I made a dash for the stairs with lamp in hand. The top step, somehow, wasn't where it should have been. I bounced merrily to the bottom, hitting each step with various well-padded parts of my anatomy. I arrived downstairs in a blaze of glory, for I still held the lighted lamp high in the air like the Statue of Liberty, as I sprawled on the floor. My downward trail was well-marked by bits of shattered lamp chimney.

After that, I stopped at the top stair and pried an eye open with my fingers to be sure that I was awake and capable of seeing where I was going. I'm still grateful to the powers that be that I didn't set the house on fire that night.

Kerosene lights were all right in their day, and so were gas lamps. But by the end of the summer, we'd decided that we'd prefer a nice little black switch in the wall with the words "off" and "on" printed on it. Thanks.

SHEEPS
IS MEAN!

When Gabriel, the Big Czech who owned the next ranch, one day bemoaned the fact that his "sheeps is mean," I chuckled up my sleeve. Some people have such a quaint way of expressing themselves. If there is any animal on this green earth that is the exact opposite of the word "mean," it is a sheep...I thought.

That was before I'd met the Big Czech's sheep.

It all started because of the water. Or the lack thereof. That was a terribly dry summer, and the water, even where it first entered Park Ditch, wasn't anything to what it should have been. And by the time it had run through fifteen miles of wandering ditches, most of it had seeped away or evaporated. Our place and the Big Czech's were at the end of the line, so what water there was left was hardly worth fighting for.

But poor old Gabe had had to fight for everything he owned in this world, and he would go on fighting until the day he died, in a strangely subtle way, of course. He'd fought to save enough money for passage to America, and after he got here he had fought to save enough money to send back to Maria for her passage. Then he had slaved in the coal mines of Crested Butte, and fought, and saved, until he had enough money to buy his ranch. And now he was slaving and scrimping and "getting ahead," obsessed by the idea that the whole world was against him, but that he would win. Fair means or foul, he would win.

He came to the door one night, dashing up on his black charger like something out of a Western, rather than driving his battered old pickup truck. His incisors gleamed white and enchanting beneath flowing mustachios. I almost loved him...until he finally arrived at the purpose of his visit. After numerous exuberant amenities, he came to the point.

"Hart," somewhere along the line he had acquired a Cockney "h" which he invariably attached to Art's name, "Hart, I vas wondering would you giff me your vater." It wasn't a question as much as a flatly stated demand, not to be refused.

Art stared at him without comprehension.

"Give you my water? What do you mean?"

"I need more vater. My crops iss burning op."

"So are mine. So are everyone's. Nobody has enough water. But I can't see why I should give you mine."

"My place iss at de end of de ditch. Dere iss not moch vater left to me."

The whining belligerence in his voice angered Art. "I know that! I don't have much either! But I fail to see why I should give you what little I have!"

"I haf more stocks to vater dan you haf, my sheeps, and my horses, and many more cows."

"Haven't you got a stock cistern that you can keep filled?"

"Shure, but..."

"I don't have a stock cistern. When the water isn't running in the ditch, I have to dip every drop out of our house cistern with a bucket."

"Yess, but it iss my spuds dat is needing vater."

"Mine do, too. I'm irrigating with what little I have, but it's not enough to help much. Say..." An idea struck Art with sudden brilliance. "Why don't we trade water? I'll give you mine for a week, and then you can give me yours. Doubling up that way will give us both enough to spread around. What do you say?"

"No, Hart. No trade. Dat iss not goot. De veek ven you get my vater, I do not get any."

"Of course not. But you have a cistern for your livestock and you could get along without any trouble at all."

"No, Hart. No trade. I vill not be vidout vater." There was a hard ragged edge in his voice that frightened me. I couldn't help feeling that it held an ominous note of warning.

"What the hell do you want, then?" Art's voice frightened me almost as much as Gabriel's. Hastily I took the children in the house and got them ready for bed. But I could still hear the men talking. "I have made you an offer of a fair trade. What else do you want?"

"Giff me your vater. You only vaste it anyway."

"Waste it? What are you getting at?"

"You let it ron on de grass."

So that was what was biting him! It was the hose sprinkling the lawn occasionally that he'd seen. By an arrangement with the force of gravity, we kept a trickle of water in the hose for various purposes, watering the stock, filling the cistern, irrigating the garden and trees, and an occasional sprinkling of the lawn.

"Why shouldn't I use it on the grass if I want to?" my better half demanded in white anger. "I pay for it, don't I?"

"But my spuds und hay is burning op!"

"So are mine!" Art was shouting by this time. "But this little trickle of a hose isn't enough to help either of us!"

"Okay, Hart," Gabe spoke with suppressed fury. "If dot's de vay you feel about it."

I came out on the front porch just in time to see him dip his hat in a bow of cold courtesy, jump on his black stallion, and gallop off.

"Of all the unlimited gall!" Art seethed. "Did you hear all that?"

"Yes." I sank down beside him on the porch step, heaving a sigh of relief. But I had a gut feeling that this wouldn't be the last we heard from old Gabe.

The next day he stopped by, his usual booming, beaming self. He carried a huge loaf of egg bread from Maria. Gabriel wasn't mad at us, after all! The bread was delicious, sweet and yellow and crusty, and sprinkled with nuts.

The next morning before Art and I had finished breakfast, Sharon came bounding into the kitchen from the yard, closely followed by Bonnie. They were exploding with excitement.

"Mommie! Daddy! Come quick and see!" Sharon squealed.

"See what?" Art was finishing his pancakes and wasn't about to be interrupted.

"Guess what! Mommie, come see! Quick, Mommie!"

"Come see!" Bonnie repeated.

I got up and both girls grabbed me by a hand and dragged me out the door.

"What in the world?" I was nonplused. Never had I seen them so excited.

"It's a hippopotamus, Mommie!"

"A....what?" I tried to calm them down. "Now listen, kiddos, hippos don't live in Colorado. What on earth are you talking about?"

"They do, too," Sharon spoke with hurt dignity. "There's a hippo in the hayfield. Just like the one in our ABC book. A real live hippopotamus. And it's moving! See?"

By this time we had rounded the corner of the house and both children pointed with sincere certainty. Sure enough, there was a... What in the world was it? It surely did look like a hippo, moving slowly through our hayfield.

Slowly it began to come apart, like pieces of a disturbed jigsaw puzzle. And I began to laugh. Even I had been fooled...for a moment.

But quickly my laughter was choked off by sudden anger. The hippo was Gabriel's sheep, turned in on our hayfield to feed. That dirty old buzzard!

Sharon looked up at me, her eyes wide with anxiety.

"Mommie? Are you mad at me?"

"No, dear," I tried to sound calm. "I'm terribly angry, but not at you."

"Are you mad about the hippo?"

"Yes, the hippo. It's not a hippo, honey child. It's Gabriel's damned sheep, eating up our hay field."

"The hippo is broken," Bonnie's gaze was still fixed on the phenomenon that was taking place. She was fascinated.

The band of sheep was beginning to scatter across the green field, eagerly gorging themselves on the choicest of our alfalfa.

"It's Gabriel's sheep!" I stormed into the kitchen, where Art was finishing his coffee. "He's turned them in to graze on our alfalfa!"

Art grabbed his hat.

"I'll chase those bloody sheep clear to Kingdom Come!" he growled as he went out the door, whistling for Buff's assistance. I hurried to the phone.

"Maria, could I speak to Gabriel?"

"He iss out somevere. I go look."

"I hate to bother you, but just tell him that his sheep are over here at our place. Could you, please?"

I hated to upset Maria, for she was an angel, with a heart as big as her entire southern exposure, and that was considerable.

"Oh, dose damn sheeps. Dey iss mean. I so sorry. I haf him come to get dem."

But the next morning, while Art was in the barn milking, I discovered the "hippo" back in the hayfield. The whole flock swept through it, chewing off the tops and trampling down the rest. Fire and brimstone blazed in my soul.

"Here, Buff!" I shouted and away we flew.

The sheep scattered before our attack like leaves in a winter wind. I howled and bellowed and yipped, running after them in a rapture of fury. Buff followed my example with great enthusiasm. The results were more than I had hoped for. The flock scattered, bleating in terror, from hell to breakfast.

Suddenly Gabriel stepped out of a patch of scrub oak along the ditch bank. His face was white with fury.

"Call off dot damn dog!"

"Get your damn sheep off our land!"

"I kill dat dog for chasin' my sheeps!"

I bit my tongue to keep from shouting that I would kill his sheep for ruining our hay. Instead I turned and walked back to the house in quivering dignity, leaving him to gather his damned "sheeps" as best he could.

For a week or more we saw nothing of the sheep. Either my screeching raid had taken some of the "meanness" out of them, or Gabriel had chosen to keep them home.

Then one afternoon I discovered our house was an island, completely surrounded by sheep. They were everywhere, in the chicken house, upsetting the turkey coops and knocking over the glass drinking fountains, tearing down last year's hay stack and snipping off my sweet peas through the front fence.

Before I could gather my wits for action against this outrage, there was a clatter of hoofs down the lane, and Gabriel came riding up on his black horse. His smile was like something out of a Gay Nineties revue. He swept off his hat with extravagant courtesy.

"Ah, Lucia, I am so sorry!" His apology was profuse. "My sheeps, dey get away again. Dese sheeps dey iss so mean. I tink I kill dem for mutton!"

Exactly my own intention, but he whirled and started after the sheep before I could tell him so. He was, however, in no hurry to get them home. He rode leisurely, this way and that, by degrees getting them together and headed the right direction. I smoldered as I watched him ride through the turkey coops, his horse's hoofs scattering the glass water fountains helter-skelter.

The children enjoyed this unexpected show immensely.

"Gabriel!" called Sharon. "What's that big sheep's name?" She pointed out a huge ram with wicked-looking horns.

"Damn 'f I know," laughed Gabriel, riding off.

"Mommie? Do you know that big daddy sheep's name?"

"No, dear."

"Damfino! He looks mean."

D amfino and I got well acquainted several days later. Again the sheep were swarming across the field. Buff and I started out on a dead run after them, barking and yelling. The ram was not one of the flock as a rule, but here he was again today, sharing in the free lunch.

The sheep fled, with Buff hot on their trail. All but Damfino. He squared off and faced me with some belligerence.

"Shoo!" I waved a stalk of hay at him as menacingly as I could. He refused to "shoo," but stood his ground, glaring at me.

"Get out of here, you blasted old fool!" I started toward him about the same moment he started toward me.

Suddenly I decided that the wisest move would be to ignore him. Turning, I left for the house. I almost reached it, too. But Damfino beat me to the gate. He struck me amidships with the force and speed of a Coney Island roller coaster. I sailed through the air for some distance before I landed, but I was still short of the gate. Every time I got to my feet to make a dash for it, he was ready for me. At last, by crawling and rolling, I gained sanctuary.

Gabriel was right. Sheeps is mean. A fine thing when they attack you on your own ranch! I ached from stem to stern.

The sheep stayed home for several days. The ditch water became nice and clear, so we decided it was a good time to fill the cistern. Art dipped out what little stale water was left, a hundred buckets or so and together we cleaned out the mud and scrubbed the walls and floor. It was a big job, but at last we finished and started the hose running to refill it.

The next afternoon, with the cistern about half full, Art went up to the head-gate on the ditch for a routine check-up. There in the middle of the ditch lay a dead sheep.

About that moment, all hell popped loose. Art, usually willing to make peace, descended upon Gabriel like an atom-buster. I never knew just what took place, but it must have been pretty fierce. That was the last time we were ever visited by Gabriel's sheep.

But Gabriel, it seemed, wanted to forgive and forget. He rode up some time later with a paper sack of green onions as a peace offering.

"It was dot ron grass dot kep' making dose sheeps come down de hill," he confided, grinning.

"How?" I asked, bewildered by his phraseology. "What do you mean, ron grass?"

"Dot grass in your yard. Ven de sheeps see it, dey ron like hell." Gabriel roared in delight at his own joke. He had made peace.

THE HIGHLY
STRAWBERRY

That title sounds a bit screwy, doesn't it? I started to entitle this chapter, The Lowly Strawberry, but thinking it over, I decided that there is nothing lowly about the strawberry except the way it grows. Everything else about it is quite highly.

Take the matter of water, for instance. The strawberry is highly sensitive to water, and/or the lack of it. Let it rain just a few drops too much, and the fruit turns to mush on the vine. But if it doesn't rain quite enough, the fruit gets temperamental and, instead of becoming red succulent berries, turns into small, wart-like knobs resembling lead musket slugs loaded with bird seed.

"Okay," says you, "what's the matter with irrigating the strawberry patch?" "Okay," says I, "we'll irrigate 'em." But the same thing holds true. Too much irrigation...an indecent kind of soup. Too little...seedy buttons, harder than the hubs of Hades. It takes a long time for a beginner to learn.

Another thing the strawberry is highly allergic to is weeds. And for some reason unknown to man, a strawberry patch attracts weeds as a magnet does pins. Not only the common garden varieties, sneeze weed, pepper grass, mustard, sweet clover, dandelion, cheat grass, wild morning glory, red root, lambs quarter, and wild oats, but also unpronounceable products of botanical imagination so fantastic that they would not dare to lift a leaf anywhere but in a strawberry bed.

And, if you've ever tried to pull up a weed which is growing right spank in the middle of a strawberry plant (and that's where they usually grow) you'll understand what I mean when I say it's highly impossible. Highly. Either one of two things happens. The top of the weed breaks off, leaving a root which will eventually send up another weed more lavish and pernicious than the first. Or, you pull up the weed with a mighty heave, and with it, the entire strawberry plant. All you have left is a yawning hole and a vast sense of frustration.

Strawberries at Park Hill were highly important because they were one of our chief money crops. At least, they were supposed to be. But the strawberry industry was off on the wrong foot, right from the start.

For the first two months, when I was running the ranch alone, I was much too busy with young calves, temperamental cows, man-eating pigs, sanguinary turkey gobblers, ad infinitum, to be able to do more than cast a hurried glance at the strawberry patch in passing.

Those two months were all the weeds needed. By the time Art arrived and we got the potatoes planted, the weeds were firmly entrenched. They thumbed an impudent nose at us, and settled back comfortably in the strawberry bed to watch us struggle. They knew we'd never win.

But we were young and ambitious and ignorant. Especially ignorant. We didn't know what lay ahead of us.

Each morning we set out with our hoes and bushel baskets in which to lug off the weeds, and the white flame of determination burning in our hearts. Each evening we staggered out of the patch with our hoes and heels dragging, and the flame extinguished. The only thing left burning was our muscles. And did they burn!

I don't know exactly how big that patch of berries was. I felt sure that it was about five acres, but Art thought it was probably a bit short of an acre. His estimates were so conservative, I snorted. At any rate, that patch was much too big, no matter how you looked at it.

We worked like devil-dogs, hoeing and pulling weeds and piling them at the side of the field in a huge stack. But the faster we worked, the faster those blasted weeds grew. Before we had worked our way halfway across the patch, the first rows were grown up again like a jungle in the back waters of the Amazon.

About the middle of June the berries started ripening, despite the weeds, and they had to be picked. That was when the fun really began.

Picking strawberries is in itself a highly specialized job. We had a book of directions that told us all about it. It said that berries picked before the heat of the day retain a better flavor, have a brighter color, keep longer, and thus command higher prices at the market. Therefore we set out to pick them before the heat of the day.

Every other day, the book said. So every other day we got up at 4:30 to pick berries. It was quite wonderful at that hour. The dawn was dawning, the robins were robbing, and the dew was so heavy and cold on everything that we were soon drenched to the skin, feeling as though we'd taken a dip in the Arctic Ocean.

About seven o'clock things start warming up. If you stop then and change into dry clothes, everything is lovely...for a while. By eight o'clock, the loveliness seems to have worn thin. By nine o'clock you don't give a tinker's hoot if the berries command a higher price at the market or not. In fact, you don't even care if they are ever picked. By ten o'clock, your back is killing you and the berries seem to be swimming about before your eyes in a kind of Jell-o-like haze. Now they are there, and now they aren't. By eleven, you are fit for a straight-jacket, as wild as an African head-hunter with termites in his trousers.

You have tried every stance known to humanity, and you still hurt. You have tried the "cave-man crouch" but your knees gave out. You have tried the "Mother Goose straddle," wherein you straddle the row with your feet planted a yard apart. This gets your picking equipment closer to the ground, a situation highly desirable. But it does something to your hip joints that is definitely not good. You have tried the "jackknife fold" which is nice for a change, but it is hard on the blood pressure in the top of your head. You can't stand that way long without busting something.

The "baby crawl" is good for a few rows. It would help if you could wear shoes on your knees. About the time those poor knees acquire the state of a pounded steak, substituting garden dirt for flour, you decide to try something else. It may be the "fanny hop," in which you sit flat on the ground, hopping and scooting along from one plant to the next. It's not long before you realize the skin you are wearing off is too valuable to be wasted this way. It's hard on trousers, too.

By now, you have but a few rows left. You should be wild with anticipation. You aren't. You are wild with misery. The only position left is the "earthworm creep." This is quite relaxing, for it is achieved by stretching out flat on your front, inching yourself forward with your elbows. It's a bit difficult to locate the berries this way, for they are above eye-level. But who the hell cares? When you are done to a turn on this side, you can turn yourself over and work lying flat on your back for a change.

By the time you have "belly-bustered" up the last row, you are ready to quit the strawberry trade, once and for all. You're through! You're washed up! Why in the devil should you kill yourself over a few crates of measly berries? Nuts to the highly strawberry!

The next morning you clean up and load the crates of berries into the back of the car. By the time you drive the fifteen miles into town, you've almost forgotten those agonized hours of screaming muscles of the day before. The man at City Market hands you a nice stack of paper money, which you promptly turn around and spend on groceries to take back to the ranch. There's even enough left to get each of the kids an ice cream cone. The berry business is not so bad after all.

In fact, the strawberry is highly profitable, if you do it right. Why else does migrant labor keep pouring across the border from Mexico?

We didn't do it right. The weeds won, eventually. We kept on struggling until we had to admit defeat. We called in the county agricultural agent for advice.

"You'll never make it," he shook his head sadly. "When pepper grass once gets a start like that, you're a gone gosling. Plow the whole patch under."

We did, berries and all. Strawberries can be highly disappointing.

CHICKEN
IN THE HAY

S pring chickens are to a ranch what firecrackers are to the Fourth of July. The latter, in each case, just isn't complete without the headaches and zoom produced by the former.

Therefore, it follows as the night the day, that we had spring chickens that summer at Park Hill. At least they were supposed to be "spring" chickens.

We ordered them in April for delivery in May. Evidently, ninety-nine percent of the poultry raisers in continental United States had done the same thing, for the hatchery wrote us that due to an overload of orders, they could make no promise as to the date of delivery. Just keep watching for them, they advised.

We kept watching for them. We haunted the mailbox. We watched for them all through the month of May. We were afraid to leave the house for fear the mail carrier would call us to announce the birth of our babies. We were afraid to go to town for fear they might be left at the mail box during our absence and perish in the hot sun.

We began to get jittery. We were like an expectant father whose baby's arrival fails to come off on schedule. We waited, gnawing our fingernails to the elbow. We had the brooder going, a fine kerosene job, with the heat radiating beautifully over a litter of clean straw. We had the water fountains scrubbed and sterilized. We were ready and waiting.

May passed and June drifted merrily on its way. But still no baby chicks. We were nervous wrecks. I would start up from my bed at night, thinking I had heard the telephone ring. At last we gritted our teeth and turned the brooder off.

The last Sunday in July, Art's folks were having a family reunion picnic. We debated long and loudly as to whether we should go and run the risk of missing the chicks. At last, our self-pity got the better of us. We had done nothing but slave since we had come to the ranch and we needed a little relaxation, we told ourselves.

And it was true, every word of it. Sunday morning we packed our contribution to the big picnic dinner into the car. We were in a dither of excitement. Our first celebration since we'd become ranchers. The kids ran around and turned somersaults on the lawn, screaming in ecstasy.

At the last minute, Art's face clouded.

"What if the chicks should come while we're gone?"

"How could they?" I argued. We'd been over all this before. "Today is Sunday. No mail delivery today, remember?" But even as I said it, a cold sick premonition began to gather in a knot in my stomach.

"The trains are still running. That is, everything but the local. They might come as far as the Junction and have to wait over until tomorrow."

He wore that white distracted look that he'd worn the night that Bonnie was born on May 1, instead of May 15 as planned, and we were in the middle of moving to a new house. I recognized it and patted his hand nervously.

"Maybe you'd better call the depot to be sure."

He did. The chickens were there.

Panic seized us. In the pandemonium that followed, we unpacked the picnic baskets from the car, packed it up again, refilled the brooder with kerosene, dropped a burning match into the straw litter and started a fire, filled the water fountains, tried repeatedly to call Art's folks to tell them not to expect us at the picnic, and scolded the children and the dog for getting under foot and tripping us.

Art leaped into the car and made the twenty-five-mile dash to the station. While he was gone, I came to the conclusion that everyone had already left for the picnic grounds in Stauffachers Grove. I gave up trying to call. They were already there, with Art's mother worrying herself sick when we didn't arrive.

Finally Art and the chicks roared up the canyon to the ranch. Tenderly, we lifted each soft yellow ball of fluff from the box, and dipped its beak in water in our best mother-hennish manner. There were one hundred beaks so it took quite a spell. We shook the dry feed invitingly before them. We set each chick where it could bask in the heat of the brooder. We did everything but diaper them and give them a bottle.

Then, with many misgivings, we departed for the picnic. That afternoon the weather turned suddenly raw and cold. It rained and hailed. When we got home that night, my heart turned sick with what we found. The brooder had gone out. After burning for weeks without a flicker, the blasted thing had failed us in our time of greatest need. For no reason at all it had gone out. Like a light.

The baby chicks were piled up in a bank in the corner, yeeping faintly and pitifully. Most of them were stiff with the cold. Those in the bottom of the pile were past redemption. They looked as though a steam roller had done them in, once over lightly. When we got the brooder going again, we tried thawing the poor babies out. About half of them showed faint signs of life.

By the end of the week, we had twenty-five chicks left. That was our "spring chicken" crop. And it was August.

They weren't big enough to be eaten until after Art left to go back to teaching in the fall. And by that time their affections had become so alienated that they no longer recognized me as their mother. At first they had adored me. Even after all the suffering I'd caused them. I felt a blush of shame every time one of them would follow me around with such loving confidence.

But when they outgrew the brooder, we moved them down to the "chicken pasture." This was a patch of sweet clover that grew higher than a man's head, and was unbelievably dense. I fed them once a day, but for the other twenty-four hours, they were on their own.

It didn't take them long to forget that they were man-made specimens of chickenhood. Nature in the raw is pretty wild. They soon resembled mountain grouse on the loose in a pine forest. My arrival in the chicken pasture was the signal for them to squawk and disappear into the depths of the jungle.

Came a day when I decided to have spring chicken for supper. It was Friday afternoon, and Art was coming over for the weekend. I was planning quite a spread. Spring chicken, roasting ears (corn-on-the-cob to the younger generation), new potatoes, cucumbers, etc., all grown on our own ranch.

I rushed down to the pasture to bag a chicken. The flock cackled and fled into the sweet clover. I wanted that chicken, so I sped in after them.

Sweet clover in October is about as sociable as a cactus plant. I beat my way through the hard dry stalks as far as I could go, but the chickens were farther from my reach than ever. They were well hidden in the far end of the pasture by the time I could extricate myself, torn and bleeding.

Nothing makes me more determined than to see my own blood flowing. I would have fried chicken that night, and nothing short of atomic disaster would stop me.

I had never shot a living creature in my life, but I had helped dress many a one Art had killed. During my callow youth I had been considered a crack shot in target practice, so I had no doubt that I could shoot the head off one of these dumb clucks with one eye shut. I ran to the house and got Art's .22 rifle.

I located a promising-looking young rooster in the weeds. Taking careful aim, I let him have it. The resulting flurry of chickens resembled a pan of popcorn when you take the lid off too soon. The flock squawked and fled in every direction. But there was no corpse.

I felt more than a little foolish. What was the matter with this old sharpshooter? But I'd be dad-burned if I'd give up on one try. I slipped around and located another cockerel. I leveled off at his eye and blasted away. Again the popcorn effect, accompanied by the mood music of two dozen squawking fowls. Again I had missed. How could I?

We would have fried chicken! I didn't see how I could possibly miss a third time. But evidently I could. I shot. No headless chicken resulted.

This time, instead of hiding in the weeds as they had been doing, they all flushed out into the open. I took one long look at the flock. I nearly fainted when the realization of what I had done began to dawn on me. There stood three roosters with blood streaming down their bibs. I had neatly drilled a hole through the wattles of each bird.

Three more shots was all it took. I had aimed too low. We had three fried chickens that night instead of one.

TO MARKET,
TO MARKET

One of the most devastating facets of ranch life is the "trip to town." If one could sink one's roots deep in the soil of the country and bask in the sunshine and showers as they come, it wouldn't be quite so bad. But one can't, it seems. It is the inevitable rushing back and forth to town, with all the attendant ramifications, that turns one into a psychomaniac. At least it did this one.

About the time you begin to get caught up on all the myriad jobs of neglected work that are piled up around the ranch premises, it's time for another "trip to town." And with another whole day sliced out of your summer, you slide back into the hole of hopeless overwork deeper than ever. You might just as well give up in the beginning. You'll never dig your way out, anyway. Every time you can almost see over the top...it's another "trip to town." You're sunk.

On "town" days you get up a little earlier, around 4:30, because there's so much extra to do. Before you can leave, there are all the regular jobs to be done: getting breakfast, milking cows, separating the milk, feeding calves, feeding pigs, feeding chickens and turkeys, washing separator and dishes, and straightening up the house a little.

After all that is done, you can devote your energies, what you have left, to getting the produce ready for market. You are usually about a week behind on your eggs, so you spend a bad hour washing dirty nasty eggs and packing them in crates. If you have a man around, it's not much of a job to load them in the car. A man can pick up a case of eggs, with a little grunting, and walk off with it. But if you're five feet tall and have to do the job alone, it's more difficult. You drag and push and heave one hundred forty-four heavy eggs up the basement stairs, get them on the kids' red wagon, and trundle them out to the car. After you've gotten the second crate loaded, you're ready for the flophouse.

But don't think you're through, yet. There's the five-gallon cream can to be taken care of. You dash back to the basement and get the heavy can out of the cooler. You stir the dickens out of the thick cream to be sure that the butterfat content is evenly distributed, then lug it up to the kitchen to clean the can. You can't take it to market with dried cream dribbling down the side, can you?

At this point, it is time to catch the kids, comb their hair, wash their faces, knees, and elbows, get them dressed up, and get your own person slicked up for public inspection. You aren't through getting your "money crops" ready to go yet, but you know from experience that perishable items will spoil in the hot car if you don't load them at the last possible moment. You also know that you'll look like a wreck, anyway, and that the children will not stay crisp and shining even for the trip to town.

But if you're a rancher, looks count for little. It matters not if your hair is windblown, if the powder has run off your face with the perspiration, if your shoes are caked with mud (or worse), or if your dress has just been torn on the corner of the egg crate. No one cares if the children are tousled and dirty. It's the produce that counts. If your berries are fresh and of top quality, no one cares that you look like the devil.

You drag a couple of crates of strawberries out of the basement and stow them in the back. There is the huge cardboard box of dressed hens which you butchered yesterday. And last of all, there is the almost immovable corpse of Brigham Young, the late turkey gobbler. You have it in the baby bathtub to facilitate transportation.

More than once, you despair of ever getting all this stuff into the limited space of the car. But at last, by dint of sheer gut power and stubbornness, you get it all in. You fill the floor space in the front seat with a five-gallon gasoline can and a five-gallon kerosene can, thrust the children into the front seat on top of your purse and jackets, slam the door, gun the motor, and tear out before anything can transpire to delay you. You're off to town! And it's not quite noon.

The trip is uneventful. You have but one flat tire, which takes practically no time at all to change. A nice man comes along just as you are finishing and offers you his handkerchief to wipe the grime from you face and hands. To be sure, there was the bumblebee that stung Sharon above the eye as she rode with her head out the window, and the small matter of Bonnie losing her balance and plunging over the back of the seat into the crate of berries. But things of that sort are to be expected.

You go first to the creamery, so as to give them time to test the cream and prepare your check before you go home. But it's no use. They're closed for the noon hour.

Next you worm your way up a dirty narrow alley to the back entrance of the café, where you will dispose of the corpse of the gobbler. The cook is busy with the noon rush and is in no mood for courtesy.

"Get out of the way, damn it!" he barks. "Can't you see this is a kettle of boiling hot grease?"

You stand around helplessly, weaving under the weight of a bathtub full of dead turkey.

"Where shall I put this turkey you ordered last week?" you inquire timidly.

"Shove it, dammit! Can't you see I'm busy?"

You shove a few dirty kettles aside and roll the turkey out of the tub on to the zinc table. You are shattered by a bellow in your ear.

"Not there, fool! Can't you see that ain't any fit place for food?"

You stand as tall as possible, trying to look cold and disdainful.

"This bird weighs thirty-five pounds," you tell the man icily. "At thirty cents a pound, you said."

"Thirty-five pounds! My God, why didn't you bring in a horse?"

"We don't butcher horses. The price, I believe, comes to $10.50."

You wait expectantly.

"Tell that to the boss. I ain't got nuttin' to do with it."

"Where is he?"

"How the hell should I know? Come back later. He's usually around."

You take your bathtub and make a regal exit, shaking with anger. Café cooks are horrid. You're so angry you almost rip the rear fender off the car while backing out of the alley.

Next you go to Lizzie O'Neill's boarding house to deliver the hens. You have covered the naked white bodies with decorum and a clean towel, but there is still a fringe of feet poking up around the box. There is nothing quite as unappetizing as the feet of a dead chicken.

Who should you meet as you stagger up the walk with your burden but Mrs. Chase, wife of the bank president! A warm rush of friendliness mingles with a sense of embarrassment. She had once sponsored a loan from the Women's Club for you when you were going off to college. You recall that she had told a friend what a lovely and promising young girl you were.

"Oh, hello!" you cry with honest pleasure, deciding to ignore the chicken feet under your nose.

She turns to stare at you, her eyebrows climbing her forehead with no recognition. You burn in humiliation. But what of it? You can't expect anyone to recognize you the way you look now.

Lizzie O'Neill looks over the hens with a piercing eye, her thin nose twitching.

"I don't like your hens!" she snaps. "They're too fat. I can't abide chicken swimmin' in fat."

"I'm sorry," you murmur in apology. But you feel she'd have kicked up a bigger ruckus if they'd not been fat.

"How much are they?" she asks, her voice loaded with suspicion.

"Six dollars and sixty-two cents. Twenty-six and a half pounds at twenty-five cents a pound." You hand her the bill with trembling fingers.

"I haven't got anything but a twenty dollar bill." She glares at you, her hands clenched on her hips. Although you can't see it, you suspect there is also a chip on her shoulder she is waiting for you to knock off. "And I can't leave. I'm makin' plum jell."

"I haven't any change with me," you offer nervously, "but if you'll trust me with your twenty dollars, I'll run downtown and get it changed for you."

"If you want your money, I reckon that's the only way you'll get it." Her tone is belligerent.

You want it, so that's the way you get it. Add on another twenty minutes.

Then you go back to the creamery and deliver your cream. There, for a wonder, they are actually friendly and courteous, and seem glad to take what you bring them, paying you without a word of complaint, after a long wait for the butterfat test. They must need the cream pretty badly. You leave with a nice little check and a little of the sting taken out of your wounds.

But salt in your wounded dignity is nothing compared to what the man in the grocery store gives you when he sees that crate of berries that Bonnie dived into. You know they're pretty much of a mess, but thought maybe he could take them home to his wife to make into jam. Besides, there's the crate of good berries.

Much, much later you emerge from the grocery store, feeling for all the world like a whipped dog with his tail between his legs. You are carrying a small box of groceries, all you get in return for two crates of berries. Some grocers don't pay cash, you find, but offer you the doubtful privilege of taking it out in credit.

Before you go to peddle your eggs and load up with grain at the poultry exchange, you go back to the café to get your money for Brigham. This time you've hyped yourself up to walk in the front door and straight up to the desk, where the boss, himself, is standing.

As he catches sight of you, he makes a rush for the kitchen, murmuring apologies as he goes. You catch something about "a hurry" and "back in a minute." You stand at the desk, awaiting his return. There are any number of legitimate reasons why a man should leave in a hurry. You study them over, wondering how long it will take him.

His daughter arrives to take over desk duties and it begins to look as though "the boss" isn't coming back. You're getting tired of standing there, and you can hear the youngsters wailing in the car out front. Tired and hungry, poor babes.

"I wonder if you could pay me for that turkey I brought in? It's $10.50."

"I'm not supposed to pay any bills. Dad does that."

"I know, but he's gone and it's getting late. I still have a long drive home tonight."

"I'm sorry, lady. But Dad will have to take care of it."

She hangs up on the receiving end of the conversation as

sharply as though she weren't standing right there before you. You stand around a while longer, beginning to feel painfully obvious under the curious stares of the eating customers. The children are squalling mightily in front of the open door.

Suddenly an idea strikes you. It will take a lot of intestinal fortitude, but it couldn't be worse than it is now. It takes but a moment to go out and get the youngsters from the car and bring them in, still howling.

You take a calm stance in front of the boss's daughter and prop your elbows on the desk, assuming an air of settling yourself comfortably for the rest of the day. The children are bellowing. The dishes on the tables shake under the impact.

Under normal circumstances, you would try your best to soothe them. But now you let them scream. It's part of the strategy.

Customers drink their soup in one gulp and rush out without the rest of their dinner. Others hold their ground but glare at you with murder in their eyes. Others try stuffing wads of bread in their ears. But it's no use. When your kids both cry at the same time, they create quite an uproar.

The boss's daughter fidgets.

"Can't you make them shut up?"

"Nope." Your answer is bland and smiling. "When they get tired and hungry like this, there isn't anything that will shut them up. All they want is their supper and their bed."

"Well..." She glances uneasily toward the kitchen. "I'll give you the money and settle with Dad later. Here!"

She hands it over much like a cowboy feeding a rattlesnake a tea biscuit. Collecting here has taken you nearly an hour. But you have your money.

When you're at last through at the poultry exchange, trading several hundred eggs for several hundred pounds of grain to produce several hundred more eggs to trade for several hundred pounds of grain, you head for the high country.

You arrive home—weary and shaken, far more exhausted than on those days when you were digging ditch. The house is dark and the kitchen stove is cold. Everyone is starved.

You long for the peace and quiet of a nice soft bed. But there are the cows to be milked, separating to be done, calves to feed, pigs to feed, chickens to feed, and the family to feed.

Ranching wouldn't be so bad if it weren't for these trips to town. Town isn't so bad living in, you ponder. But it's sure hell going to!

FAREWELL,
GOOD EARTH!

When school started in September, Art joyfully renewed his contract. I couldn't leave when he did, for I had to harvest the garden, dispose of the chickens and turkeys, and arrange to leave the place in someone else's hands.

As he bid me a fond farewell and drove off that day, leaving behind the agonies of ranching, his face was lighted with a boyish glee as exuberant as when he had first arrived.

He was free! Free from temperamental cows. And troublesome neighbors. And hungry calves. And man-eating pigs. And persnickety chickens. And vicious turkeys. And thieving sheep. And dozens of cats. And ditch digging. And water fights. And gopher holes. And runaway horses. And millions of weeds. And bottomless mud. And back-breaking strawberries. And gasoline lamps. And hand-drawn water. And snapping, snarling customers.

He was free!

Freedom is a wonderful thing. He would be able to stay in bed until seven o'clock in the mornings. He'd have nothing to do but sit around at school all day, teaching. And after dinner there'd be nothing more strenuous than the easy chair, his slippers, and the evening paper. Ah!

He'd had enough of the Marlboro Man and the simple life. He'd had his education in that field.

If you yearn to "get back to the basics" all I can say is—go for it! It's an education.